Woodcarving in the Scandinavian Style

Harley Refsal

 Sterling Publishing Co., Inc.   New York

Edited by Laurel Ornitz

Library of Congress Cataloging-in-Publication Data

Refsal, Harley.
    Woodcarving in the Scandinavian style / Harley Refsal.
      p.   cm.
    Includes bibliographical references and index.
    ISBN 0-8069-8633-6
      1. Wood-carving—Norway. 2. Wood-carving—Sweden. 3. Wood-carved
figurines—Norway. 4. Wood-carved figurines—Sweden. I. Title.
TT199.7.R44   1992
736′.4′0948—dc20   92-16979
                                        CIP

10 9 8 7 6

Published in 1992 by Sterling Publishing Company, Inc.
387 Park Avenue South, New York, N.Y. 10016
© 1992 by Harley Refsal
Distributed in Canada by Sterling Publishing
℅ Canadian Manda Group, P.O. Box 920, Station U
Toronto, Ontario, Canada M8Z 5P9
Distributed in Great Britain and Europe by Cassell PLC
Villiers House, 41/47 Strand, London WC2N 5JE, England
Distributed in Australia by Capricorn Link Ltd.
P.O. Box 665, Lane Cove, NSW 2066
Manufactured in the United States of America
All rights reserved

Sterling   ISBN 0-8069-8633-6

Acknowledgments

The Swedish Institute (Stockholm), Döderhultarn Museum (Oskarshamn), Norwegian Foreign Ministry (Oslo and New York), Norwegian Folk Museum (Oslo), Viking Ship Museum (Oslo), Nordmanns-Forbundet (Oslo), Norway-America Association (Oslo), Maihaugen (Lillehammer), Akademiet (Rauland), E.L.C.A.–Faculty Research Grant (Chicago), Sons of Norway (Minneapolis), American-Swedish Institute (Minneapolis), Vesterheim (Decorah), and Luther College (Decorah) have all provided me with financial and/or moral support in connection with my research. To them as well as to my family, friends, and countless other museum staffers, librarians, and woodcarvers, I extend my sincere appreciation.

Except where noted otherwise, all of the photographs were taken by Chip Peterson (or me) and all of my carvings were painted by my wife, Norma Refsal.

CONTENTS

Color section follows page 32.

PREFACE

In this book, the discussion of Scandinavian-style figure carving, and "flat-plane" carving in particular, will deal with a style of carving that developed and became popular in Norway and Sweden. Although Denmark, Finland, and Iceland also comprise part of Scandinavia, I am limiting the discussion to Norway and Sweden, since their conditions and traditions are fairly similar—especially, as we shall see, when it comes to figure carving. Therefore, in the context of this book, the term "Scandinavian" will refer only to Norway and Sweden. The style of figure carving I will be discussing was common in both countries, but it was far less common in Denmark and Finland and nearly nonexistent in Iceland.

The term "flat-plane" carving stems from a particular style of figure carving—one in which large, flat planes, created by using primarily a knife and perhaps just a gouge or two, were left intact. Smooth, rounded sculpting and sanding were typically not employed in the final finish.

I was introduced to Scandinavian figure carving during my first visit to Norway in 1965. Two years later, while studying at the University of Oslo, I was able to travel more widely throughout Norway as well as in Sweden. Since I had worked with wood and also done some whittling as a boy, I became interested in the woodcarving traditions of both countries. I was especially intrigued by the small wooden figures I saw in shops and museums.

Upon returning to the United States in 1968, I began to carve figures of my own, using a pocket knife and a wood chisel that my father, a carpenter and farmer, had made from a worn-out file. Since I was unable to locate any carvers creating the style of figures I had seen in Scandinavia, I simply gleaned what information and inspiration I could from photos, articles, and sketches I had made.

One of the articles I eventually ran across featured photos of some carvings by Axel Petersson Döderhultarn, whose rough-hewn figures have made a lasting impression on me. Using only a few well-placed cuts and leaving large flat planes, he was able to convey fascinating stories in wood.

I had been attempting to tell stories through my figures too, and Döderhultarn's style of carving provided just the means of expression I had been seeking. I began using this style of carving to create objects and figures with which I was familiar, and I began trying to say more by saying less.

Since that first visit in 1965, I have travelled in Norway and Sweden on many occasions. By the early 1980s, however, I noticed that fewer figures carved in this flat-plan style were available in shops.

Meanwhile, I had been carving a great deal in the United States and teaching courses and workshops on Scandinavian-style figure carving since the early 1980s. So when my family and I moved to Norway in 1988, where I was enrolled in a graduate program of folk-art studies, I was eager to explore the figure-carving tradition further. I also hoped to locate carvers who were still creating figures in this style. But I eventually learned that the tradition had become almost extinct, and I couldn't locate a single course being taught on the subject, either in Norway or Sweden.

Therefore, when I was asked if I would teach a week-long course at the school I was attending, I readily accepted. Since 1988, I have taught numerous courses and workshops in Norway on flat-plane carving and am pleased to see that there is now a growing number of Scandinavian as well as American and Canadian carvers who are carving once again in that style.

During the year my family and I lived in Norway, I travelled t Norway and Sweden, gathering additional information tradition and its practitioners. I am happy to be able to share what I have learned with you in this book.

After having taught courses throughout the United States as well as in Scandinavia, I can't decide which I enjoy more: carving figures myself or trying to help others develop their skills so that they can tell their own stories in wood. But I *can* say with certainty that my admiration for the small wooden figures that whispered into my ear over twenty-five years ago only keeps on growing.

—HARLEY REFSAL

THE HISTORY OF SCANDINAVIAN FIGURE CARVING

1

Viking Era and Medieval Carving

Before focusing our attention on Scandinavian figure carving, it is important to consider the general context in which this particular folk art emerged. As we shall see, wood chips were flying in Scandinavia long before figure carving became popular there.

Our earliest examples of woodcarving in Scandinavia date back to the Viking era (ca. 800–1050 A.D.). Already back then, woodcarving had reached a high level of achievement, as indicated by the items found buried with the Oseberg Ship, now housed at the Viking Ship Museum in Oslo. The Oseberg Ship was named after the Norwegian farm that was on the land from which the ship was excavated. Buried with the ship were vehicles and furniture and all kinds of household and personal items. Thus, the excavation, conducted in 1904, yielded a unique look into the past, providing us with a time capsule thought to date from the first half of the ninth century.

The items decorated with carving include the ship itself, a horse-drawn carriage, and three sledges. In terms of the motifs, there are relief-carved animal ornamentation, geometric designs, and some three-dimensional figure carving. The high quality of the carving from the Oseberg excavation suggests that woodcarving must have been a leading form of art in the Viking era.

Another excavated Viking ship, the Gokstad Ship, can also be seen at the Viking Ship Museum. Dating from around 900 A.D., this ship also contained some carved items,

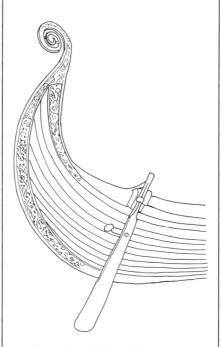

Oseberg Ship (Viking Ship Museum, Oslo).

including parts of a bed frame that features the relief-carved head of an animal, possibly a horse. In addition, the head of an animal or beast of some kind, carved three-dimensionally, appears on one of the ship's oarlocks. Both the bed frame and oarlock were rendered in a mode of carving that has become known as the Borre style. Named after a burial mound on a Norwegian farm called Borre, this style was widespread both in Norway and Sweden.

Wooden stave churches (named for the large staves, or pillars, in their support structure), built in Norway from ca. 1000 to 1300 A.D., also featured examples of woodcarving. Of the estimated one to two thousand stave churches once found throughout the country, only about thirty have survived. But decorative carving from these churches provides us with yet another excellent source of Norway's rich carving heritage. Animal and plant motifs, especially around doorways and on pillars, were common. The motifs often blended native and foreign elements, drawing some of their impulses from classical traditions common throughout other parts of Europe.

The carving found on stave churches as well as from earlier Viking era ship finds was undoubtedly done by trained artists, some of whom may have worked under royal patronage. As the stave church era progressed, local carvers may have also been trained on site to do some of the carving, but most of the work from this period was done by specialists, not by "common folk" who simply picked up a tool and began to carve.

The tools available to Viking era carvers certainly must have included gouges and curved knives in addition to simple straight-carving, or all-purpose, knives. It is impossible for the intricate relief work found in the Oseberg excavation as well as on stave church portals and doors to have been done using only a knife. A woodcarving tool from the Middle Ages found in an excavation near Tønsberg, Norway, suggests that a

Relief-carved head on a bed frame, from the Gokstad Ship (Viking Ship Museum, Oslo).

which were undoubtedly of cultic or religious significance, have been discovered. Also, a few gaming pieces, such as the carved-ivory chess pieces known as the Lewis Chess Set (now in the British Museum in London), have been found. But, in the main, the carving during the Viking era was decorative or applied art on functional objects.

It is of course possible that carved wooden objects, including figures, were far more common than the evidence suggests. But due to the nature of the material, wood, most would have rotted away long ago. However, one excavation site at Kvivik on the Faroe Islands, settled by Scandinavians during the Viking era, has yielded two tantalizing wooden horses and two small wooden boats, probably created for use as children's toys. One can only speculate about the identity of the carver or carvers of these objects. The simplified, almost crude, pieces could certainly have been carved with only a knife, so perhaps just a "common person," handy with a knife, created them.

On the whole, however, the rich carving tradition, practised in Scandinavia approximately seven

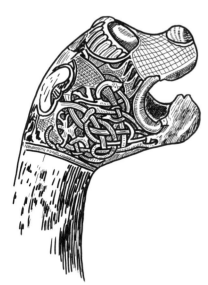

Animal head post from the Oseberg find (Viking Ship Museum, Oslo).

were available several hundreds of years earlier as well.

There is very little evidence of "art for art's sake" from the Viking era. Some small figures, carved primarily in bone, ivory, or stone,

wide variety of tools had been developed and were available to carvers at that time. Therefore, we must conclude that similar tools

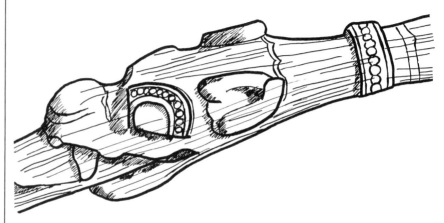

Oarlock from the Gokstad Ship (Viking Ship Museum, Oslo).

hundred to a thousand years ago, was carried on by trained artists. Yet, as we shall see, their work lived on to inspire countless self-taught craftsmen, who studied the Viking era and medieval motifs and began replicating them on their farms and in their homes.

From Stave Church to Storehouse: The Emergence of Folk Art

Scandinavia, along with much of the rest of the world, was ravished by the Black Death, or bubonic plague, in the mid-fourteenth century. It is estimated that over half of the population died, after which large parts of Scandinavia, especially Norway, were laid waste for several generations. Artistic development was severely curtailed, as the people were devastated and had to spend virtually all their time simply eking out a living. It wasn't until a couple of centuries had passed that the people were back on their feet to the extent that they could think about devoting time to aesthetically enhancing their surroundings.

The populations of Norway and Sweden have historically been overwhelmingly agrarian. Only a very small percentage of the people lived in towns, a situation that remained true well into the nineteenth century, when the Industrial Revolution began to create jobs in factories. Prior to that, most people lived on self-sufficient farms, where all their buildings, vehicles, tools, furniture, and utensils were made of wood, right there on the farms.

Borgund Stave Church, Sogn, Norway, ca. 1150.

At least well into the eighteenth century, Scandinavian farmers were largely illiterate, had no formal art training, lacked travel opportunities, and had few if any pictures or books at their disposal. So, farmers who wanted to decorate a building or household object turned for inspiration to designs they saw firsthand in their own communities. In some parts of Sweden, inspiration could have been drawn from nearby manor houses or castles. In other parts of Sweden as well as in Norway, inspiration often came from

Detail from doorframe, Gol Stave Church, ca. 1200 (Norwegian Folk Museum, Oslo).

Viking era carver (drawing by Uwe Rudolf).

churches. After viewing a professionally carved candle holder, baptismal font, pulpit, or portal, countless farmers returned to their homes and modelled drinking vessels, candle holders, utensils, or other household objects on what they had seen. In Sweden and especially in Norway, with its numerous ornately carved stave churches, farmers began to replicate pillars and doorways from churches on their storage buildings, virtually all of which were made of logs. Carved ornamentation also began to appear on their houses.

In addition to scroll-like plant motifs and geometric designs, majestic and daunting images of animals figured prominently in architectural carving. Lions were especially common. Originally a symbol of kingship in the Orient, the lion motif made its way, with returning Crusaders, to the European continent, where it became a common element in heraldry. Over time, the theme was picked up by other artists on the Continent, including carvers, and eventually lions found their way into Scandinavian design—first as deep-relief carvings mounted on doorposts of stave churches and later on storage buildings, furniture, and tools.

This phenomenon of untrained artists adopting the designs and motifs of earlier artists and then reinterpreting and creating them in their local setting is a good ex-

Carving tool from the Middle Ages, found near Tønsberg, Norway.

ample of what we now call "folk art." Folk art was also referred to as "peasant art" earlier in this century, since it was typically made by rural folk, of meager means, who had to create and decorate their possessions themselves, rather than purchase them. In the

Piece from the Lewis Chess Set, made of walrus ivory, 1200s (British Museum, London).

Scandinavian context, folk art was basically the art used on utilitarian objects, including everything from buildings and vehicles to utensils and toys, that was created by the people in the general population, who drew their inspiration from the designs they saw around them.

Two main types of art existed simultaneously during this "Golden

Another piece from the Lewis Chess Set.

Age of Scandinavian Folk Art" (ca. 1700–1850). Urban or "international" art thrived among the rather small upper class, while more of a peasant art flourished in the heavily populated rural areas.

It is of interest to note that from the sixteenth through the eighteenth century, farmers and other rural craftsmen who were creating folk art had relatively few tools at their disposal. Specialized tools for carving, fine woodworking, and joinery were jealously hoarded by the small groups of urban craftsmen, most of whom were in the guild system. In Norway, a royal decree from the Danish king (Norway was under Denmark from 1380 to 1814) actually made it illegal for farmers throughout the country to use refined tools. In an effort to thwart competition with the trained craftsmen of the government-controlled guild system, farmers were forbidden to use tools other than knives and axes—tools deemed sufficient for basic but rough construction of log buildings, simple furniture, and farm implements. Many farmers obviously ignored the decree, which was in effect for about a hundred years, from the late seventeenth to the late eighteenth century, and made or bartered for fine woodworking tools. Still the ban was somewhat effective, and much of the work done by rural craftsmen during that era reflects the limited range of tools at their disposal.

However, if one has only a cou-

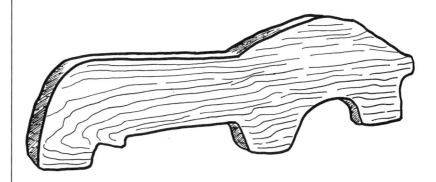

Kvivik horse from the Viking era, Faroe Islands.

St. Göran, Lögdö Chapel, Medelpad, Sweden, early 1500s.

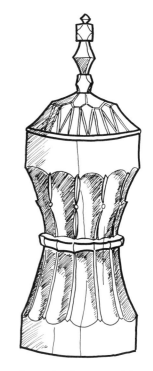

Carved wooden baptismal font from Telemark, Norway, Middle Ages.

ple of tools available, one can develop amazing skill with just those tools, and some highly impressive work was created during that period with just a knife and axe. The story is told in the Norwegian county of Telemark about a man who was seeking employment as a log builder. Having just wandered into a community, he was directed to a site where a log building was under construction. The man approached the foreman about a job, but the foreman was hesitant and asked the stranger if he could handle an axe. Without saying a word, the stranger walked over to a chopping block, spread apart the fingers of his left hand, and laid it palm-down on the block. He then proceeded to chop into the block four times, striking the axe perfectly in the spaces between his outstretched fingers. When he was finished, the foreman said, "You can start right over there on the far corner!"

Kubbestol (chair made from a hollowed log), Hallingdal, Norway, before 1873.

Wood: The Universal Material

Norway and Sweden are richly endowed with forests. Nearly half of Sweden and a quarter of Norway are covered with pine, spruce, and birch. Due to the cool climate afforded by the Scandinavian peninsula's northerly latitude, trees grow slowly and are typically not harvested until they are seventy-five to one hundred and fifty years old. Annual growth rings are therefore close together, providing ideal material for woodwork of all kinds.

Almost everything was made out of wood in traditional, rural Scandinavian society. In addition to buildings and vehicles, objects that we today regard more as hardware items—such as hinges, pails, tools, and fencing materials—and even shoes—were made primarily from wood.

Instead of searching for a tree that would provide that "nice, straight board," farmers and craftsmen often chose a suitably

Contemporary rendition of traditional Norwegian knife and sheath, made by Norma Refsal, 1989.

curved or twisted piece instead. A branch from a gnarled mountain birch tree that had been deformed through years of buffeting by wind and snow might yield just the perfect shape from which a hinge, C-clamp, or plow beam could be made. A naturally bent limb, with the grain following the shape, is of course stronger than a piece of wood that one could craft into that shape artificially. Thus, a plow beam made from a six- to seven-inch-thick, naturally bent birch branch fitted with an iron tip proved to be nearly as strong as one made entirely from metal.

Burls were also widely used. The grain in a burl does not run in only one direction but appears to swirl around almost randomly, so burls provided ideal material from which to carve bowls and scoops.

Craftsman with knife and axe.

Bent birch tree.

C-clamp, made from a naturally formed piece of birch (Øyfjell, Norway).

Bowls were often turned on a lathe, but free-form shapes were also created, carved from a crotch or burl. Ale bowls, sometimes carved in the shapes of hens or geese, were used for ceremonial drinking, especially in connection with weddings, funerals, and other ceremonies or festivities. Some bird-shaped ale bowls were carved with rounded bottoms, and they would be floated on the surface of the ale in a larger wooden container. They served as floating dippers, from which one could either drink directly or pour the ale into another container.

Due to their ceremonial use, ale bowls were frequently decorated with carving or painting. Other bowls, however, were often shaped according to the piece of wood from which they were carved, with the shape itself providing the design.

Horse hames or other harness fittings and parts were also made using naturally bent or curved pieces of wood—preferably birch, because of its strength—and were frequently decorated as well. The harness saddle shown here, originally from a farm in the Swedish province of Ångermanland and now on view at the Nordiska Museet, Stockholm, is a good example of the use of a naturally curved piece of wood. A component of the harness also exemplifies the use of the lion motif that was mentioned earlier.

Clogs, or wooden shoes, provide yet another example of articles commonly made from wood. Although we associate wooden shoes primarily with Holland, clogs have been worn since the Middle Ages in many parts of Europe, including Norway and Sweden. Even after the introduction of the more expensive leather boots and shoes,

Chip-carved decor on a house in Gudbrandsdalen, Norway (Maihaugen, Lillehammer).

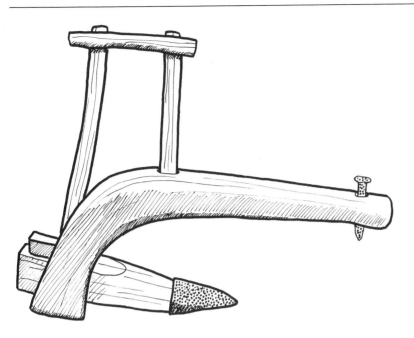

Wooden plow with iron plowshare (Norwegian Folk Museum, Oslo).

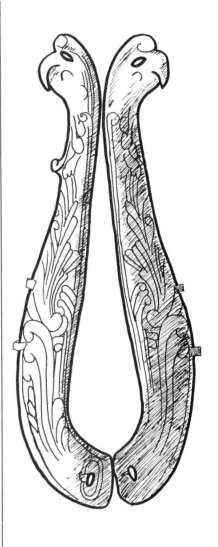

Horse hames from Småland, Sweden (Nordiska Museet, Stockholm).

Ale ladle from Setesdal, Norway (Norwegian Folk Museum, Oslo).

wooden clogs continued to be popular since they could be made locally and were so convenient. You simply stepped into them and walked off. Clogs were often lined with hay or straw, both for cushioning and for warmth. The pair pictured here, believed to have been made in Scandinavia and brought to the United States by immigrants who settled near Hoffman, Minnesota, were even fitted for winter traction, complete with

Wooden shoes, with metal spikes on the bottom.

Lion detail on portal of Eidsborg Stave Church, Telemark, Norway, ca. 1300.

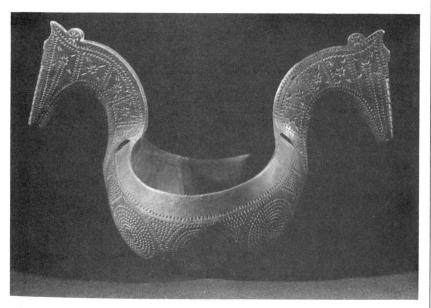

Norwegian ale bowl, possibly late eighteenth century (Vesterheim/Luther College Collection, Decorah, Iowa) (photo: Darrell Henning).

hand-forged metal spikes on the bottom.

Many of these articles, intended for everyday use, were decorated. Employing chip carving, relief work, incised carving, and/or wood burning, traditional craftsmen transformed hinges, drinking vessels, ladles, and harness parts into articles that were also aesthetically pleasing. "The eye also has its needs" is an expression that craftsmen regularly took to heart.

As we can see, even though it is difficult to document a figure-carving tradition *per se* within Scandinavian folk art that goes back more than a few hundred years, the stage had been set long before. Wood had been a universal material for centuries. It would only be a matter of time before craftsmen familiar with the material and skilled with knives would begin turning their attention to carving objects other than just utilitarian items.

Harness saddle from Ångermanland, Sweden (Nordiska Museet, Stockholm).

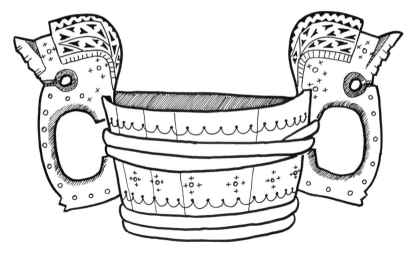

Container from Sogn, Norway, decorated with a combination of wood burning and chip carving.

The Emergence of Carved Figures

The earliest carved human or animal figures in this folk-art tradition were probably used as protective or good-luck charms. Some were mounted inside houses, whereas others stood guard in storage buildings.

Two figures from a farm called Heggtveit Vestre in Telemark, Norway, are noteworthy examples of such charms. One of the figures, a *husgud* (house god), approximately six inches tall and featuring the head of a human, was originally fastened high up on the interior wall of the house. Believed to date from the Middle Ages, it is one of the oldest and finest examples we have of a house god in Norway. It resembles the kind of figure, perhaps a saint, commonly found on walls or pillars inside churches.

The second figure, a horse and rider, pictured here, was prominently placed as a protective or good-luck charm on the second floor of the Heggtveit farm's storehouse. The 1830 date painted on the horse's stomach, together with the rider's dress, suggest that the figure represented a government official or military man, perhaps attached to the Telemark Company in nearby Dalen. In 1830, Swedish military uniforms were being worn in Norway, since Norway was united with Sweden from 1814 to 1905. The rider's outstretched hand has a small hole drilled through it, indicating that some object, perhaps a flag on a flagpole, was originally part of the carving.

A candle holder in the form of a lion, now in the Sandvig Collection at Maihaugen in Lillehammer, Norway, harks back to the lion motif that was mentioned earlier. The piece was originally from a farm near Ringebu in Gudbrandsdalen.

Another figure in the Maihaugen collection, an elegant horse, made by the famous eighteenth-century carver Kristen Erlandsen Listad (1726–1802), is technically a toy but one of those toys that children undoubtedly had to handle very carefully. The Listad horse was featured in a commemorative stamp in 1987, the one-hundredth anniversary of the Sandvig Collection.

Another horse pictured here was carved in approximately 1825

Horse and rider, 1830 (Lårdal Bygdemuseum, Telemark).

Listad horse from the late 1700s, Maihaugen, Lillehammer, as depicted on a commemorative stamp.

Candle holders from Östergötland, Sweden (Nordiska Museet, Stockholm).

Horse from Morgedal, Telemark.

Candle holder from Ringebu, Gudbrandsdalen, Norway, now at Maihaugen, Lillehammer.

Horse carved by Anne Hellem, ca. 1825 (Gransherad Bygdemuseum, Telemark).

by Anne Hellem of Gransherad, Telemark. This carving, also undoubtedly created for use as a toy, is fairly unique in that it was made by a woman. Carving as well as woodwork in general was typically done by men, whereas women devoted themselves more to textiles.

The carving of wooden animals and human figures by common folk in Sweden is traceable back more than two hundred years. It can readily be documented since about 1840, with the emergence of the now-world-famous Dalecarlian horse, an object that has become Sweden's unofficial national symbol. The province of Dalarna, and especially the community of Mora, had long been a center for the building of wooden clock cases, and the horses whittled from the scraps left over from the clock cases gradually became an economic mainstay for countless families.

Even earlier than the 1840s, however, men working in lumber camps often lived far back in the woods and were separated from their families for weeks or months at a time. As a way of using their free time during the long winter evenings and in order to be able to bring home toys for their children, the men often whittled horses or other figures. Although roosters and pigs were not uncommon objects, horses were favored by carvers as well as by the children who received them. These figures, some of which can be seen in the Nordiska Museet in Stockholm and in various provincial museums, were painted in colorful floral motifs or sometimes left un-

Toy horse from Øyfjell Bygdemuseum, Telemark.

The world-famous Dalecarlian Horse.

painted. The horse from Dalarna shown here was originally painted, but years of use by small hands have nearly obliterated the coloration and given it a warm, dark patina.

As previously mentioned, it was near Mora that large-scale production of the Dalarna figures began in about 1840. The carving of the figures, primarily horses, was done by local craftsmen in their homes. Working in pine or spruce, a good carver could produce a dozen horses per day, using a hatchet and knife as his only tools. Flat-plane carving, with visible tool marks, was the result. The figures were usually left unsanded.

The painting was done by specialists, who often drew their inspiration for designs from the horses featured in the well-known wall paintings in the area. Many of these wall paintings seem to have received *their* inspiration from illustrations in the so-called "Gustav Adolf's Bible" of the

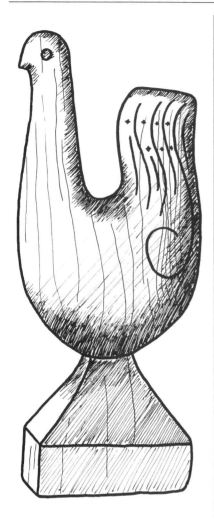

kets, or spinning wheels, they typically had along a good supply of carved horses, which they used as payment for their room and board. The figures thus became a kind of currency. Frequently the horses, which were meant to be used as toys, were given to the children of the farmer or innkeeper with whom they stayed. In addition to paying for lodging, the horses were also commonly traded for such items as seed or wool. Upon returning to Mora, the craftsmen in turn sold the goods for cash.

Frequently other salesmen would come to Mora and buy up large quantities of carved horses to use as gifts, barter items, or payment for room and board, as they travelled throughout the country selling their wares. Although it is not known exactly how much they had to pay for the horses, it was at any rate cheaper for them to pay for their lodgings with wooden horses than to use cash, and apparently the horses were readily accepted as payment wherever they travelled.

Demand for the horses became so great, therefore, that large-scale production became common—even in the 1840s. As noted earlier, the carving was done by craftsmen, and specialists did the paint-

Rooster from Dalarna, 1840s (Nordiska Museet, Stockholm).

1580s. The styles of saddles and martingales as well as the combination of colors chosen by the painters of the wooden horses suggest that wall paintings significantly influenced many of the painters.

It is interesting to note that as long ago as the 1840s the Dalecarlian horse had already become a popular item throughout Sweden. When Mora-area craftsmen travelled by horse and wagon to other parts of the country to sell their locally produced clocks, bas-

Horse from Dalarna, 1840s (Nordiska Museet, Stockholm).

ing. Anders Nisser, the son of the well-known, early twentieth-century painter Mor Nisser, estimated that he had to shoot as many as fifteen to twenty squirrels per year, just to keep his mother supplied with enough squirrel hair to make the brushes she used to paint the horses.

The production of Dalecarlian horses has continued right up to the present. Since 1928, nearly all the figures have been made in and around the village of Nusnäs, near Mora. Although modern technology is now used both in sawing out the figures and in some aspects of the painting process, each figure is still carved by hand by local craftsmen and receives its painted decoration by hand as well. Not only are the horses sold in Sweden and throughout the rest of Europe, but they are sent to shops in Japan, Australia, Canada, and the United States.

It is clear that there has been a folk-art tradition of carving small human and animal figures for at least the past two to three hundred years, especially in Sweden. Three-dimensional figures were sometimes created as part of a decorative whole (lions on doorposts, for example). Other figures were carved as free-standing utilitarian objects (toys, human figures used

Doorframe detail on storehouse, Telemark, ca. 1300 (Norwegian Folk Museum, Oslo).

as candle holders, bird-shaped drinking vessels, and so on). Still other figures were created as pieces of representational, non-functional art, but they were prob-ably made by carvers who found figure carving to be nothing more than an enjoyable pastime. And then along came Axel Petersson Döderhultarn. . . .

2

FIGURE CARVERS

Axel Petersson Döderhultarn

Axel Petersson has been called a natural genius. He was born in the parish of Döderhult near Oskarshamn in 1868. His figures, which typically depict the peasants and village folk around whom he grew up and lived, have earned him the reputation of one of Sweden's greatest artists.

Even as a boy, Petersson exhibited considerable artistic talent both at home and in school. His talent was never encouraged, however, and his only training stemmed from a brief informal apprenticeship under a local woodcarver and sculptor, Edward Källström. His primary interest lay in whittling or sculpting small figurines, an activity considered a worthless pastime by his neighbors as well as his family.

His family finally decided that the young Axel should emigrate to America, where he would be forced to stand on his own two feet and make something of himself. So money was provided, and off he went. But he didn't get farther than nearby Malmö, where instead of purchasing a ticket to America he spent most of his travel money on lottery tickets and partying.

Upon his return to Oskars-

Axel Petersson Döderhultarn (Döderhultarmuseet, Oskarshamn) (photo: Ataljé Lindblad).

hamn, where his widowed mother had moved in 1889, he continued his figure carving. Much to the dismay of his family and acquaintances, carving remained his primary activity. For nearly twenty years, he lived in relative isolation, venturing out only occasionally to attend social gatherings or to sell his inexpensive wooden figures at the local market in Oskarshamn.

As he had been taught by Källström, Petersson carved in a rather naturalistic style during the beginning of this period. His early work, often in pear and rendered in quite a traditional style, was typically sanded. Although the style of his work defies a systematic chronology, some time around 1900 he developed more of a rough-hewn, flat-plane, or minimalist style. Using a knife and just a few gouges, he began carving figures in alder. Upon completion, many of his figures were then painted in subdued colors.

Petersson's six- to fifteen-inch-tall figures portray local peasants engaged in everyday activities: milking a cow, attending a funeral, wedding, or baptism, having their picture taken by a photographer, and so forth. It's been said that he also derived inspiration from medieval wooden sculptures in churches, caricatures drawn by the famous Swedish artist Albert Engström, and illustrations in various publications, including some that were Norwegian.

In 1909 Petersson was invited to participate in a caricature exhibition in Stockholm. Public response to his work was immediate and overwhelming. In the newspaper *Dagens Nyheter* (*News of the Day*) on January 20, 1909, art critic Georg Nordensvan wrote: "Axel Petersson's old men are irresistibly amusing. They depict

Peasant (The American-Swedish Institute, Minneapolis, Minnesota).

such primitive art as one could wish for, made out of a couple of simple contours using only a couple of strokes, but, from an artist with sure eye and nimble hands. It is a new conception with a personal touch . . . small masterpieces of complete nonconformative art." As can be said of a great

cartoonist or caricaturist, he had mastered the difficult art of simplification—saying more by saying less.

Following closely on the heels of the exhibition in Stockholm, some of his figures were purchased by Swedish art museums, lending even further legitimacy to the artistic merit of his work. He also began receiving requests to have his work exhibited throughout the rest of Europe and in the United States. Hailed as "Döderhultarn" (the man from Döderhult), he started using that name in addition to Axel Petersson.

In 1910 his work was shown in Paris. In 1911 it was exhibited in Brighton, Copenhagen, Rome, Turin, Stockholm, and Malmö. Fifty-seven figures were also shown in Oskarshamn, and a museum association was formed there to lay the groundwork for a Döderhultarn Museum. In 1912 some of his work was shipped to the United States, where the Swedish Consulate sent it on a tour of several cities, including New York, Buffalo, Toledo, Chicago, Boston, and San Francisco.

Döderhultarn's prominence as a "high artist" is well documented and accepted. However, at the same time that his work was being exhibited internationally and purchased by museums, he continued to carve figures for local sales.

The photo of the two boys outdoors with the carved wooden figures on page 28 is from the archives of the Döderhultarn Museum and is believed to have been taken in 1913. The photo suggests that the boys were using the wooden figures as toys. The two human wooden figures clearly appear to be the work of Döderhultarn. The photo had been mailed, without an accompanying

Finger Hooking (The American-Swedish Institute, Minneapolis, Minnesota).

Detail from Finger Hooking.

note, to Döderhultarn, possibly as a way of thanking him, or as proof that the figures that had been ordered had arrived and were indeed being used.

Beginning in 1908, Döderhultarn's figures were sold through the Handcraft Association in nearby Kalmar. The store continued to serve as his local sales outlet, even after the artist had achieved international fame.

A postcard sent to Döderhultarn by the store in 1915 features a photo of the store's interior, showing several of the artist's carvings on the counter. On the back of the postcard, the store placed yet an-

The Christening (The American-Swedish Institute, Minneapolis, Minnesota).

Detail from The Christening.

Boys playing with carved wooden figures, including two of Döderhaltarn's. Photo from the archives of Döderhultarmuseet, Oskarshamn, ca. 1913.

Army Horse, by Döderhultarn (The American-Swedish Institute, Minneapolis, Minnesota).

other order with the carver. Individual figures sold for approximately ten *kronor* (U.S. $1.50–$2.00), while groupings sold for thirty to forty *kronor*.

Photos of Döderhultarn's figures were widely circulated. Articles about, and reviews of, his exhibitions often included drawings of his work, and postcards featuring his carvings were available at least as early as 1912, if not earlier.

It has been said that Döderhultarn was unique. It seems that his uniqueness lay not in that he was one of the first to carve figures in this style, but rather in that he was the first essentially self-taught figure carver to be accepted or discovered by the art world. Döderhultarn stood firmly planted in the world of folk art, carving wooden figures destined for use as children's toys—but he also carved similar figures for exhibition in art museums and galleries throughout Europe and America.

Döderhultarn's Influence on Other Carvers

Döderhultarn's influence on other carvers should not be underestimated. Since photos and drawings of his work were so readily available and widely circulated, they undoubtedly served as inspiration for countless other carvers in Scandinavia and abroad.

A "Döderhultarn figure" became a generic term for any small wooden figure rendered in a minimalist style. For example, a souvenir stand near Oskarshamn hung out a sign some years ago advertising "Döderhultarn figures." When asked if the figures for sale were

"Döderhultarn" i sin Atelier.

Oskarshamns Kulturnämnd

Döderhultarn in his studio (Döderhultarmuseet, Oskarshamn) (photo: Ataljé Lindblad).

actually carved by Axel Petersson, the proprietor replied that, of course, they weren't carved by Axel Petersson, but because of the style and subject matter, they were indeed Döderhultarn figures.

The simplicity of Döderhultarn's figures comprised an art form with which common folk could easily identify. The people, who had grown up in a tradition in which practically every male was at least somewhat skilled with a knife, apparently felt that they too could create "Döderhultarn figures," even though they may not have had any art training. For instance, in a letter to Döderhultarn in 1922, a resident of a home

for the elderly in Sundbyberg, Sweden, wrote that he was looking for a hobby to help pass the time. Since he had done some woodworking years ago, he said, he was interested in working in wood, perhaps in making some small figures. Then he went on to ask for Döderhultarn's assistance and advice.

The popularity of Döderhultarn's figure carving among common folk quickly spread beyond his own country. Evidence of this can be seen from an article in the September 28, 1913, issue of the widely read Norwegian magazine *For Bygd Og By* (*For Country and Town*), which described the work

of a figure carver named Ragnvald Einbu from Gudbrandsdalen. The writer, apparently without any need for further explanation to the general readership of the magazine, compared the Norwegian artist to "the well-known Axel Petersson, Döderhultarn, from Småland in Sweden."

Another Norwegian, Sverre Johnsen (1844–1939) created, among other pieces, Döderhultarn-style figures. According to the *Lexicon of Norwegian Artists*, Johnsen was called "Norway's Döderhultarn." Johnsen was, however, only one of many who carved small individual figures or groupings depicting such themes as a drinking party, card players, or a chorus, and was compared to Petersson.

In the United States and Canada, where hundreds of thousands of Norwegians and Swedes had emigrated only a few decades earlier, figure carving had also become popular. Dr. Marion Nelson, professor of art history at the University of Minnesota and former director of Vesterheim, the Norwegian-American Museum in Decorah, Iowa, wrote in 1989: "In doing research . . . it became evident that there was a lot of small figure carving among the Norwegians in our area about 50 years ago. The subjects were immigrant[s] and pioneer[s]. . . ."

Despite the lack of written documentation indicating that Döderhultarn's carvings directly influenced other carvers, several of his subjects and designs can clearly be recognized in the work of later carvers, One is obviously Oscar Sjögren, an artist who emigrated from Emmaboda, Sweden, in the 1920s and settled near Duluth, Minnesota. Not only did he create figures in a style reminiscent of Döderhultarn's, but he featured some of the same subjects, such as a wedding scene and a photographer.

Photos and sketches of pieces by H. S. "Andy" Anderson, the well-known American caricature carver, suggest that he too had seen pictures of Döderhultarn's work. Anderson, in turn, went on to influence other American figure carvers, including Harold Enlow. Enlow states that when he began carving, his initial inspiration came from Anderson's book, *How to Carve Characters in Wood.*

Although many carvers drew much of their inspiration from Döderhultarn's work, this should not minimize in any way their own creativity and artistic talent. Everyone derives inspiration from one source or another. As I have mentioned earlier, Döderhultarn's work has served as an inspiration for my own work as well. It is merely interesting to note that

Hobo, by C. J. Trygg.

his influence has been enormous and far-reaching—right up to the present.

Petersson was once asked how he felt about other carvers emulating his work. Did he mind? Did he regard them as unwelcome competition? No, he said, he wasn't threatened in the least. "There are thousands of snuffbox carvers out there, but there is only one Döderhultarn!"

A Sampler of Nineteenth- and Twentieth-Century Figure Carvers

Carl Johan Trygg

It has been said that it's often only fate that determines which artist becomes the standard-bearer of a new style of art. Axel Petersson became known as the father of "Döderhultarn figures," but perhaps the figures could have been called "Trygg figures" instead.

Born in 1887 in Skagerhult, near Örebro, C. J. Trygg began carving wooden figures as a boy. As one of nine children in a poor family, he had to quit school and leave home at the age of twelve to earn money to supplement the family's income. But he continued to carve rough-hewn figures that depict the types of folk he knew from his background: primarily Swedish farmers, laborers, preachers, policemen, and seamen.

Even though C. J. Trygg began carving figures before Döderhultarn's 1909 Stockholm exhibition, the figures of Trygg, who was nineteen years younger than Döderhultarn, were similar in style to Döderhultarn's and extremely well done.

At first Trygg was unable to make a living from just the sales of his carvings and had to carve on a part-time basis while working at other jobs. But eventually, perhaps in part because of an exhibition of

Detail of Hobo.

his work in Stockholm in 1915, he was able to devote himself full-time to his carving.

Trygg enjoyed telling a story about the initial purchase of his

Detail of Hobo.

work by an art dealer in Stockholm. The dealer's wife had wanted her husband to purchase a dozen figures, but the dealer only purchased three. The next day, Trygg, who had never met the art dealer in person, dressed up in his finest and went to the shop, where he promptly bought all three of his own figures. The day after that, the dealer contacted Trygg and ordered two dozen figures. Through the years, this dealer continued to be Trygg's best customer in all of Stockholm.

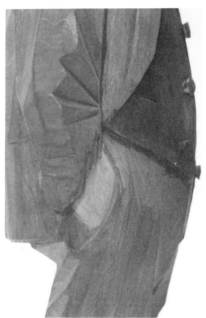

Detail of Hobo.

Together with his three sons, Carl Olof, Nils, and Lars, who were also figure carvers, Trygg emigrated to Canada in the 1930s. There, C.J. and sons, especially Carl Olof (born 1910), apparently met with considerable success. While their figures had been earning them only a few crowns each in Sweden, they were fetching up to $20 apiece in Canada.

Logger, dated 1930, by C. O. Trygg.

Both C.J. and C. O. Trygg eventually returned to Sweden, however, where they continued their careers. C.J. is said to have carved well over ten thousand figures before his death in 1954. Much of the Tryggs' work can be found in private collections in Canada and the United States as well as in Sweden.

Sailor, by Lars Trygg.

Oscar Sjogren

Born (Josef Oscar Sjögren) and raised near Emmaboda, Sweden, Sjogren (1883–1964) emigrated to Superior, Wisconsin, in 1922. He was employed as a commercial

At the Fishmarket, by Sjogren (from the collection of the St. Louis County Historical Society, Duluth, Minnesota) (photo: St. Louis County Historical Society).

artist in nearby Duluth, Minnesota, but woodcarving was his lifelong passion. Drawing on memories of friends and neighbors back in Sweden as well as folks from the Duluth–Superior area for his models, Sjogren was yet another carver who created figures in a minimalist style.

Although his figures are somewhat more refined than those of Döderhultarn, they clearly show knife-and-gouge marks and portray some of the same rural characters and situations featured in

Detail of Logger.

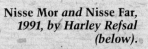
Another Season, 1984, by Harley Refsal.

Nisse Mor and Nisse Far, 1991, by Harley Refsal (below).

Dancers, by Axel Petersson Döderhultarn (Döderhultarmuseet, Oskarshamn) (photo: Sven Nilsson).

The Christening, by Axel Petersson Döderhultarn (The American-Swedish Institute, Minneapolis, Minnesota).

Three Women Having Coffee, by Herman Rosell (The American-Swedish Institute, Minneapolis, Minnesota).

B

The Dalecarlian Horse.

The Tomte, 1991, by Harley Refsal, painted by Karen Jensen.

Wedding, by Axel Petersson Döderhultarn (Döderhultarmuseet, Oskarshamn) (photo: Sven Nilsson).

C

The Knife Makers, 1989, by Harley Refsal (photo: Arne Aas) (below).

The Emigrant, 1989, by Harley Refsal (photo: Arne Aas) (right).

Farmer, 1987, by Harley Refsal.

Taming the Prairie, 1987, by Harley Refsal (from the collection of H.M. the late King Olav V of Norway) (photo: Arne Aas).

D

Peasantry Wedding, by Oscar Sjogren (from the collection of the St. Louis County Historical Society, Duluth, Minnesota) (photo: St. Louis County Historical Society).

The Man with the Spade, by Sjogren (The American-Swedish Institute, Minneapolis, Minnesota).

The Male Chorus, by Sjogren (The American-Swedish Institute, Minneapolis, Minnesota).

The Man with the Spade (closeup).

The Photographer, by Sjogren (from the collection of the St. Louis County Historical Society, Duluth, Minnesota) (photo: St. Louis County Historical Society).

Paul Bunyan, by Sjogren (from the collection of the St. Louis County Historical Society, Duluth, Minnesota) (photo: St. Louis County Historical Society).

Döderhultarn's pieces. His work is represented in numerous private and museum collections. The largest collection of Sjogren figures and groupings is owned by the St. Louis County Historical Society in Duluth, Minnesota.

Herman Rosell

Herman Rosell (born 1893) was another self-taught Swedish carver who created small figures and groupings that depict rural life in the nineteenth century. His abili-ties as a carver and caricaturist were highly regarded, and in addition to participating in exhibitions both in Sweden and abroad, his work was featured in a film on Swedish television in 1959.

Although his subject matter is

Three Women Having Coffee, by Herman Rosell (The American-Swedish Institute, Minneapolis, Minnesota).

Fiddler and Woman, by Rosell (The American-Swedish Institute, Minneapolis, Minnesota).

similar to Döderhultarn's, his style of carving is more refined. Rosell has stated that he became familiar with Döderhultarn's work only after he had carved for many years and developed his own style.

In addition to pieces in Sweden, a number of Rosell's figures can be seen at the American-Swedish Institute in Minneapolis, Minnesota.

Emil Janel

Born Emil Nygård in 1896 near Orsa, Sweden, this gifted artist began to attract attention even as a very young boy, when he started whittling small wooden animals. Despite a lack of any formal training, he continued to carve and paint, and at nineteen years of age was awarded first prize at a national sculpture exhibition in Stockholm.

Recognizing his artistic abilities, both Carl Milles, a well-known Swedish sculptor, and Anders Zorn, a painter, invited Emil to study with them. But the young artist's parents would not allow it, stating that he had to help his father with his job as a woodcutter and part-time ranger.

In 1923 Emil travelled to Winnipeg, Canada, where he joined his brother and began working as a lumberman. Eventually he moved to Seattle and then to San Francisco, where he lived for the rest of his life. It was when he moved from Canada to the United States that he adopted the surname "Janel," after the famous turn-of-the-century sports figure John L. Sullivan. He had been told that his Swedish name, Nygård, was too difficult and confusing for non-Scandinavians to pronounce.

Working primarily in un-

Sven and Urban Gunnarsson

When Sweden's late Prime Minister Olof Palme visited Cuba some years ago, he brought along a gift for Fidel Castro. It was a small wooden caricature of the bearded Cuban leader, carved by Sven Gunnarsson.

Gunnarsson (1909–1985), the son of a furniture maker, began carving figures as a boy, and in the late 1930s, his hobby also became his career. His rough-hewn, flat-

Immigrant Couple, by Rosell (The American-Swedish Institute, Minneapolis, Minnesota).

Gunnarsson Seaman.

seasoned alder, Janel carved his fifteen- to twenty-four-inch figures using only a mallet, gouges, and a knife, holding the figures between his knees. As with Döderhultarn's and other Scandinavian figure carvers' work, with which he undoubtedly was familiar, Janel's characters, typically tall and thin, depict common folk going about their everyday activities. Frequent subjects were laborers, immigrants, and loggers he had encountered. However, he did not carve in an angular, flat-planed, minimalist style, but rather his work has been categorized as "exaggerated realism."

During the first years he lived in the United States, he had to earn part of his livelihood from jobs other than his carving. But eventually he supported himself through his carving alone, especially after he began his association with Maxwell Galleries of San Francisco. In 1965 Janel was awarded the Royal Order of Vasa by His Majesty King Gustav Adolph VI of Sweden in recognition of his work as an artist. He died in San Francisco in 1981.

Man with Cap, by Gunnarsson.

Martin Engseth

Born in Norddal, Møre-Romsdal, Martin Engseth (1903–1972) emigrated from Norway to America in 1926. In addition to working as a *rosemaler* (rose painter), Engseth also carved figures, much in the spirit of other figure carvers of the time in Norway, Sweden, and Scandinavian America.

plane figures depict rural folk, laborers, and clearly recognizable political leaders.

In the 1960s Gunnarsson was joined by his son Urban, who began carving on a full-time basis when he was fifteen. Urban, who carves in a style similar to that of his father, who died in 1985, continues the tradition at the family's shop on Drottninggatan in Stockholm. The figures, carved in basswood, are painted by Urban's mother, Ursala.

Seated Man, by Emil Janel (The American-Swedish Institute, Minneapolis, Minnesota).

Bjarne Walle

From the outset of his adult life, Bjarne Walle (1911–1989) wanted to make woodcarving, especially figure carving, his career. Although his flat-plane figures sold for more than 30,000 *kroner* ($4,000–$5,000) at his first major exhibition in 1945, the artist from Bamble, Norway, also had to work as a carpenter. His desire to tell stories, however, both through his

Saturday Night, by Bjarne Walle (from the collection of Svein Romtvedt, Telemark, Norway).

carved figures and his writing, was so strong that he often carved or wrote during his lunch breaks. It was not until 1970 that his income from figure carving and writing allowed him to devote himself full-time to them.

Walle's painted figures, typically larger and less angular than

The Woodchopper, by Engseth (photo: Darrell Henning).

those of Döderhultarn, often feature trolls or people in humorous situations. His carvings, as with the many stories and books that he wrote, usually have "happy endings." It's been said that Walle couldn't bring himself to allow bad things to permanently befall his characters.

Henning Figures

A carver of trolls, Norwegian rural folk, Vikings, fishermen, animals, and characters from Nordic mythology, Henning Engelsen (born in 1918) lives at Kapp, in Toten, about 120 kilometres north of Oslo. He has been creating his flat-plane "Henning figures" since 1947.

The Wood Gatherer, by Engseth (photo: Darrell Henning).

Fisherman—Henning figures.

Milking Time—Henning.

Miner—Henning.

His basswood figures, which are popular souvenir items, are sold in shops throughout Norway as well as abroad, and especially in the United States. The Henning staff includes about a dozen people, a third of whom rough out the figures by machine. Surface carving is then done by hand by another group, after which the pieces are painted.

Other Carvers

The list of carvers whose work has just been reviewed does not even presume to be complete but merely provides a sampler. Figure carvers such as Gudleik Brekhus, Styrk Fjose, Ragnvald Einbu, Axel J. Persson, Sverre Johnsen, L. Larssen, Hans Sorken, Telle Rudser, "Ole the Hermit," John Al-

tenborg, "Grandma Larkin," and countless others could have been included as well.

By the early 1980s, most of the figure carvers who had been working in Döderhultarn's style back in the 1920s and 1930s—probably the height of its popularity—were no longer alive. Only a few bearers of the flat-plane, Döderhultarn-influenced tradition remained.

Figure carver Aslak K. Svalastoga, Rauland, Telemark (photo: courtesy of Rauland Dansarring).

Sveinung Svalastoga: porch pillar at Svalastoga home, Rauland, Telemark (photo: Norma Refsal).

Carving by Olav Bakken, Gransherad, Telemark.

Lady with Goat, by Olav Tveito, Vinje, Telemark (Lårdal Bygdemuseum, Telemark).

Telemark Cow, by Bakken, Gransherad, Telemark.

Closeup of woman.

Man carved by Anton Pearson, Lindsborg, Kansas (The American-Swedish Institute, Minneapolis, Minnesota).

Woman carved by Pearson, Lindsborg, Kansas (The American-Swedish Institute, Minneapolis, Minnesota).

The Tippler (closeup).

The Tippler, Vesterheim, Decorah, Iowa (carver and date unknown).

The Tippler (rear view).

Norwegian Packhorse, by Sjur Mørkve, Voss, Norway (from the collection of Nils Kjome, Decorah, Iowa).

Carving by Kolbein Hommedal, Indre Arna, Norway (from the collection of Nils Kjome, Decorah, Iowa).

Horse from Småland, Sweden.

My Own Carvings

The New Schoolmaster, 1988.

This is a turn-of-the-century immigrant named Oskar. (Carving instructions are in Chapter 3; the pattern is in Chapter 4.)

Ringer, 1988.

Chiseled, from pine, using only a hatchet (1988).

Father Christmas, 1988.

Kenneth and Julie Boots: Wedding Day, 1941 (carved in 1991).

Horse and Rider, 1988.

The Ice Fisherman, 1990.

Heading Home, 1988.

Skiing, 1990.

Martin, 1988.

Swedish Rooster (inspired by original, from 1840, in Nordiska Museet, Stockholm), 1988.

Woodcarver, 1990.

Nobel Peace Prize–conference ale bowl, 1991 (Luther College, Decorah, Iowa).

Another Season, 1984.

CARVING A FIGURE, STEP BY STEP

In the following step-by-step photos, you'll see how a figure is carved in this flat-plane style. Front and side-view patterns of the figure, a turn-of-the-century immigrant named Oskar, can be found on page 96.

Pattern size as shown can be adjusted by enlarging or reducing the pattern on a copying machine. Cut out the pattern, making paper templates of the front and profile views.

Using the templates, I traced the designs onto a 3″ × 4″ × 8″ piece of seasoned basswood. Then I sawed the rough shape (both front and side views) on a band saw. Most of the carvers mentioned earlier used this same technique before beginning to carve their figures. Others, however, roughed their figures to shape with a mallet and gouge or a hatchet.

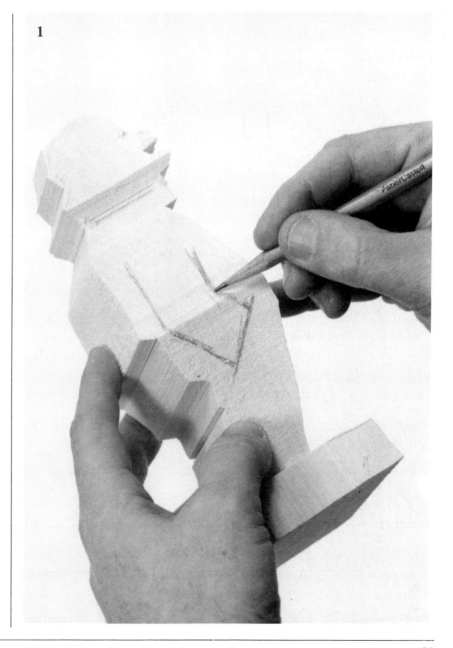

1

Draw lines to indicate placement of his right arm. Remember to leave the arm plenty wide.

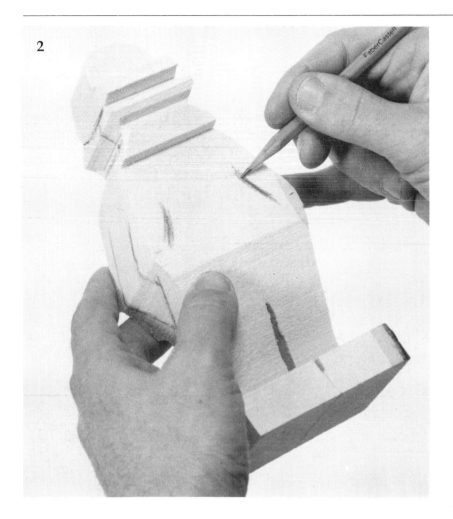

2

Draw lines to locate the opposite arm. Make sure that both arms are similarly positioned and of equal width. Look at the figure from above to ensure approximate symmetry.

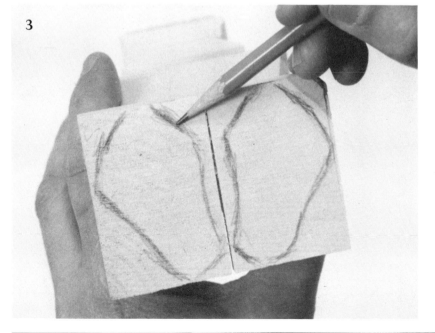

3

Lines may also be drawn to indicate placement and shape of the feet. Note that people usually stand with their heels close together and their toes pointing outward. This gives the carved figure greater stability and also adds visual interest, preventing a rigid, static appearance.

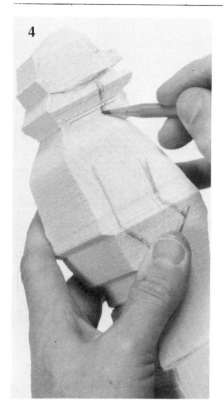

Indicate placement of the cap and hair. Again, remember to check for symmetry.

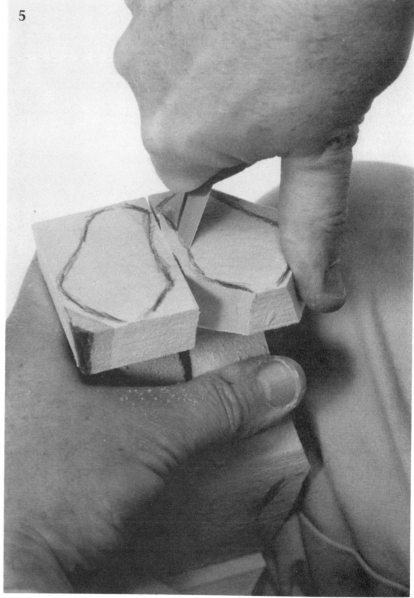

Using a standard fixed-handle bench knife (sometimes also called a carving, whittling, or sloyd knife), begin by removing stock from the outside of the heels and around the shoes, following the shapes drawn on the bottom.

6

Remove all the stock around the shoes.

Using the tip of your knife, slice in towards the body along the lines drawn to indicate arm placement.

7

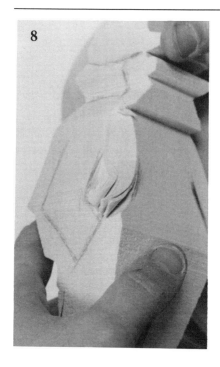

8

Here your goal is to remove stock from in front of and behind the arm, both to free the arm and narrow his chest. Avoid prying out chunks or slices of wood with the knife tip so that it doesn't snap off.

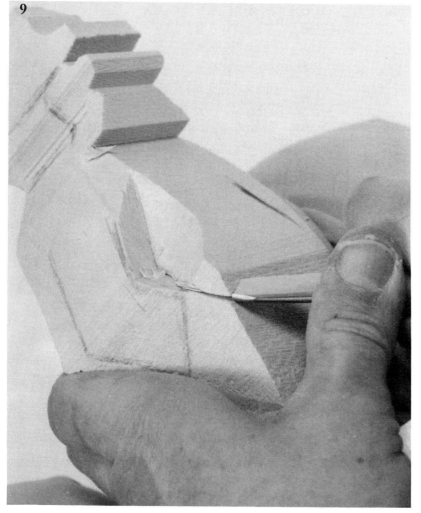

9

Slice, don't pry. Note that I hold the knife in my right hand (my power hand) and press on the back of the blade with my left thumb, as I slice through the wood. This technique gives me a great deal of cutting power while maintaining good control. Very little pressure is being applied with my right hand (it is primarily holding and steering the knife), while my left thumb is supplying most of the muscle. If you have never used this technique before, practise on a scrap of wood to perfect the technique before starting on a figure. Hold the knife in your power hand and the piece of wood in your other hand. It may seem awkward at first, but most carvers find that once they have perfected the technique, they have additional power as well as better control.

*Repeat the same procedure behind
the arm (steps 10–14).*

11

10

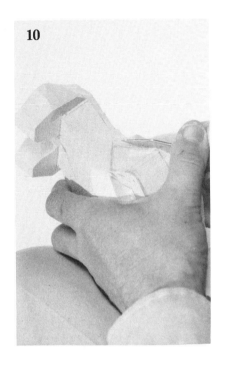

12

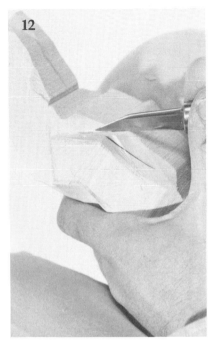

14

*With the tip of the knife, cut along
the line drawn for the pocket. Then
surface the arm.*

13

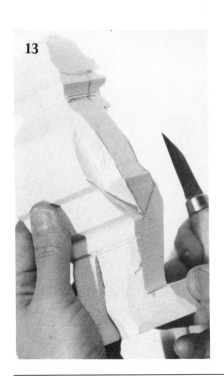

15

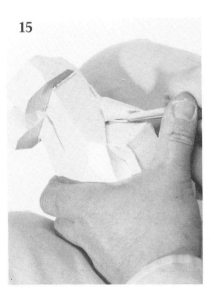

Cut a fold in the shirt sleeve at his elbow (steps 16–18).

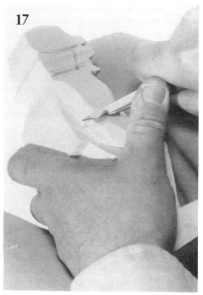

17

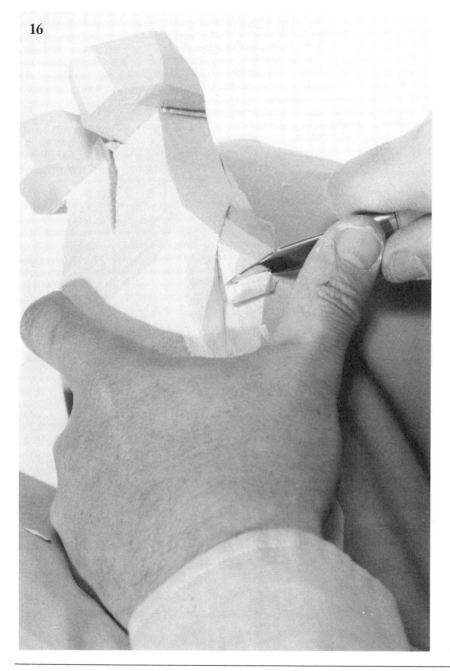

16

18

19

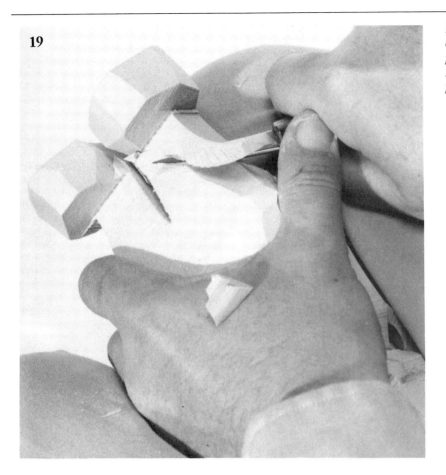

Begin to shape the leg. In this style of carving, I don't want to create a perfectly rounded cylinder for the leg; instead, I try to leave large, flat planes.

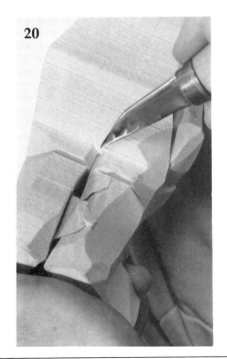

20

21

The shaping cuts simulate creases in his trousers (steps 20 and 21).

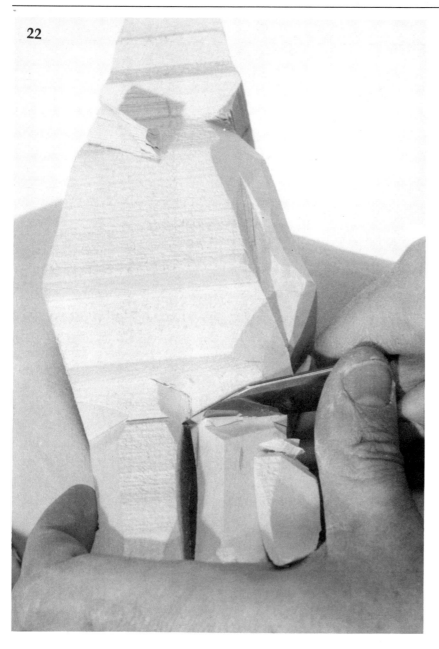

22

After shaping the back of his trouser leg, make a deliberate V-cut to form the crease behind his knee.

23

The trouser cuff is formed with a V-cut. First, make a stop cut . . .

. . . then cut perpendicular to the leg to form the V-cut.

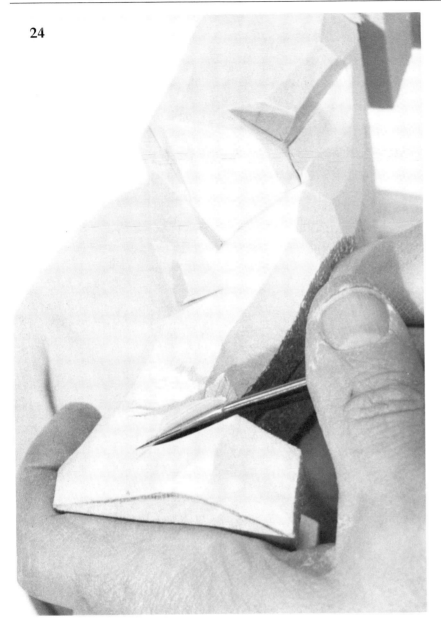

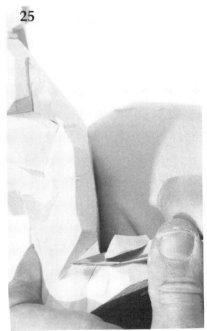

25

Shape and thin his shoe . . .

26

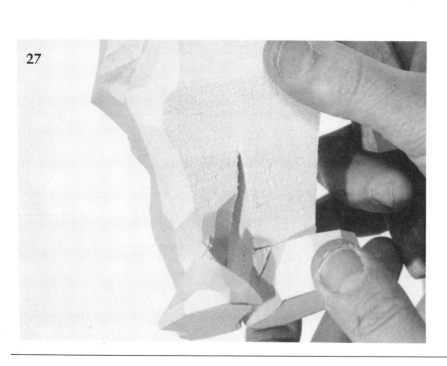

. . . leaving it the full width at the sole (steps 26–28).

28

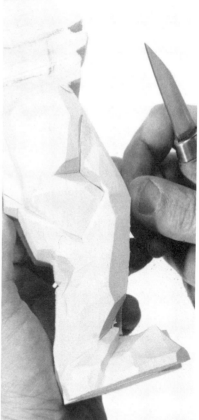

27

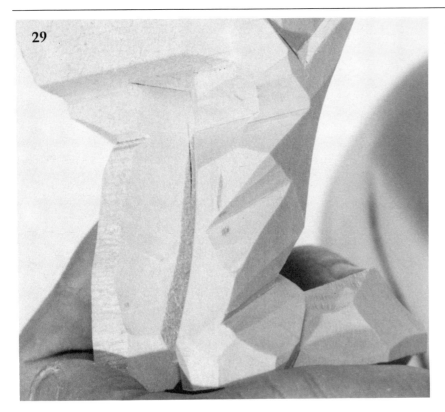

A large V-cut between the shoe and knee creates another interesting wrinkle.

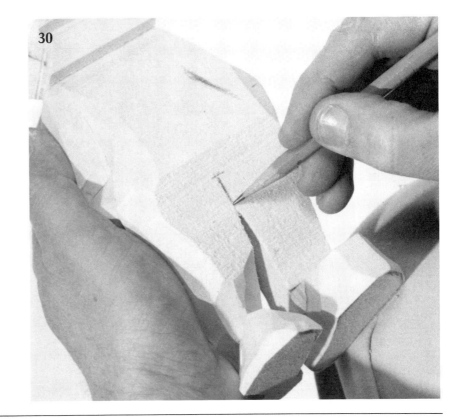

Pencil in a vertical line to indicate how high the crotch of his pants will go.

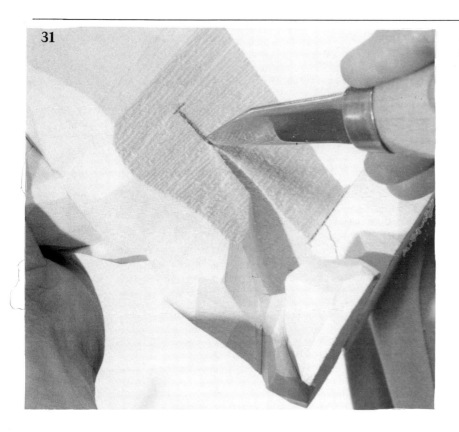

31

Holding the knife like a pencil, cut along the line.

32

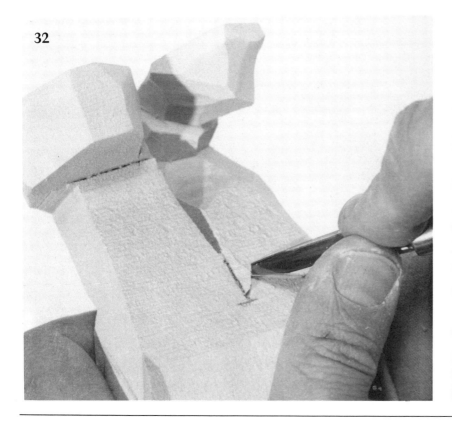

Starting at the top of the vertical line, slice downwards (steps 32 and 33).

33

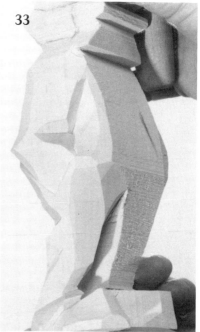

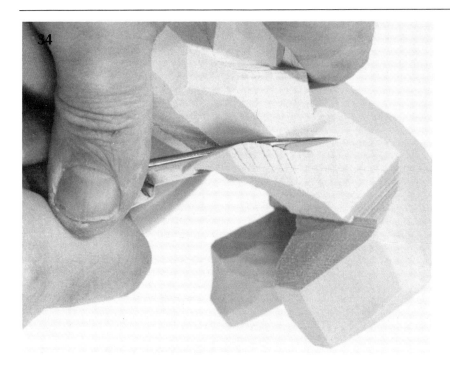

Repeat the same procedures for the leg, shoe, and arm on his left side. As you proceed, turn the figure every now and then to make sure that it stays fairly symmetrical—the arms should be approximately the same width, the angles of the pockets should match, and so forth (steps 34–45).

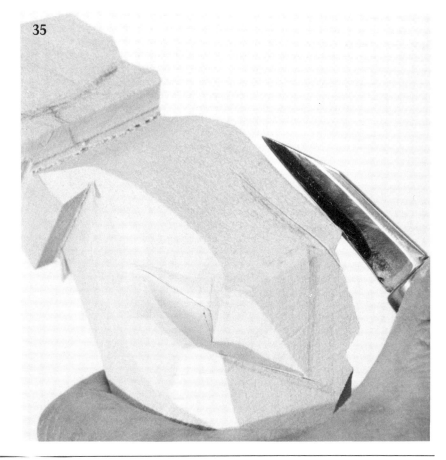

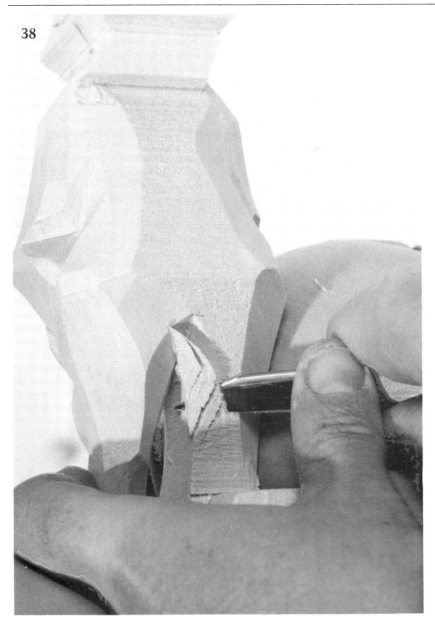

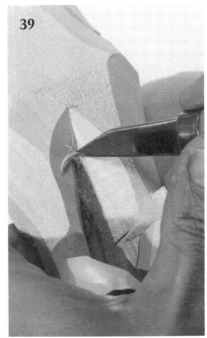

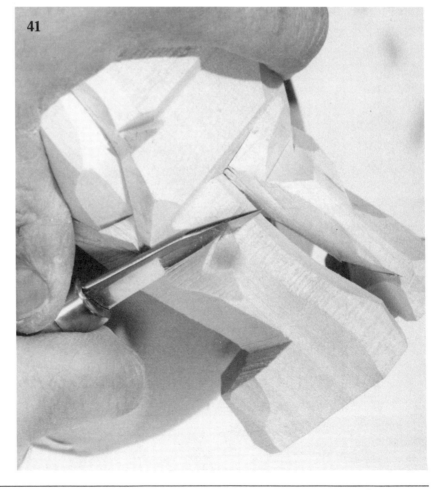

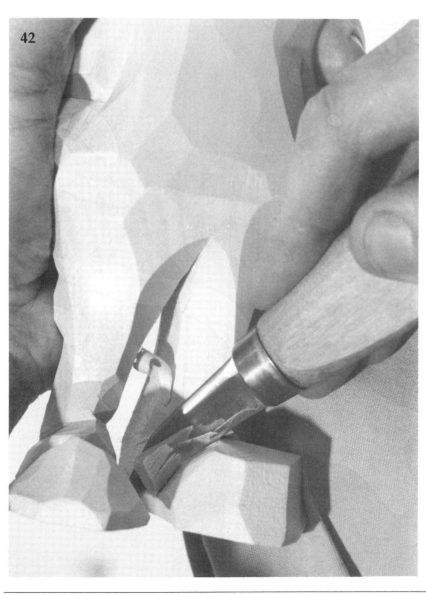

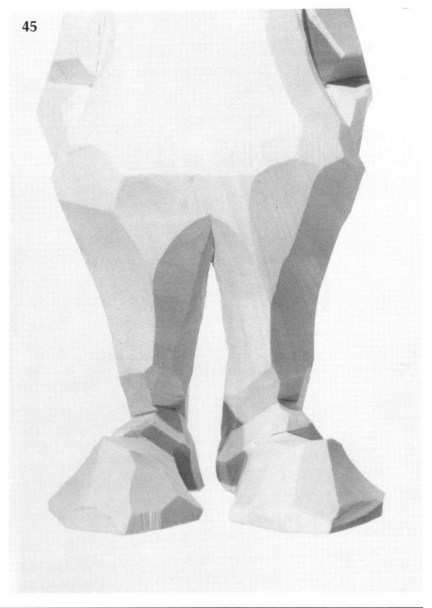

46

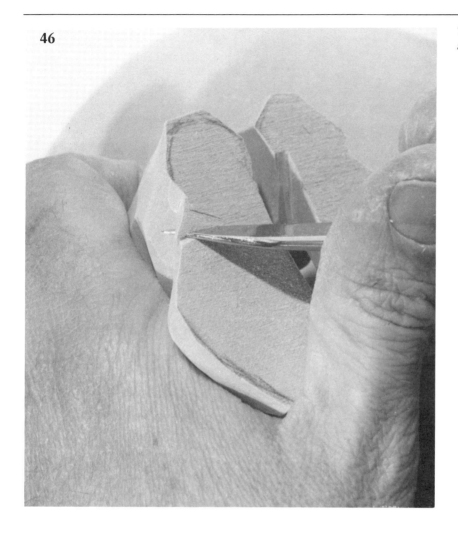

To form heels, notch in from both sides of each shoe.

47

Remove a bit of wood (¹⁄₁₆″ is enough) from the edges of the bottom of his shoe soles (steps 47 and 48).

If you stand the figure on a hard surface, you can see that the shadow effect created by slightly turned-up shoe soles "lifts" the figure. This relieves him of what would otherwise be a static, "nailed-to-the-floor" appearance.

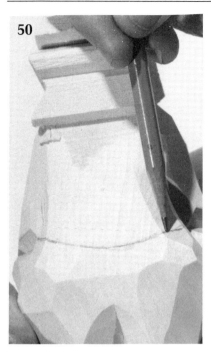

Pencil in a line, both in front and back, to mark the location of the bottom of his sweater vest. Avoid perfectly horizontal lines.

Recess wood below the sweater, making it appear to have some bulk (steps 51 and 52).

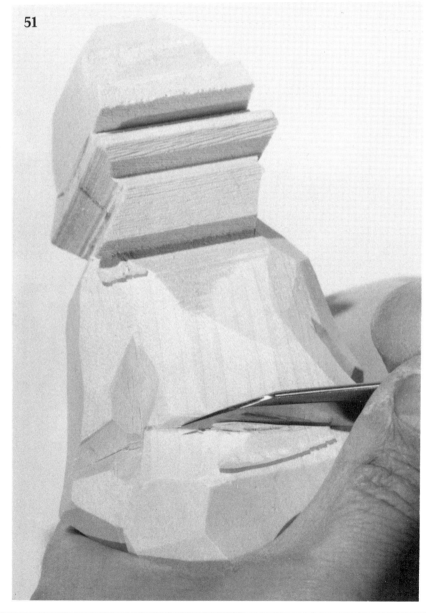

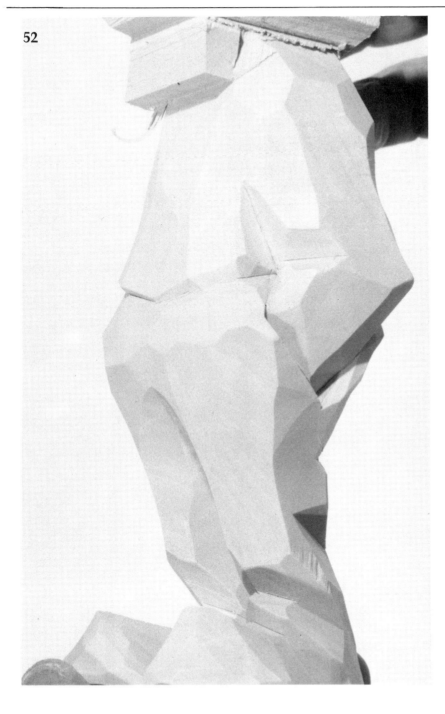

52

53

Surface the rest of his body . . .

. . . stopping at his head.

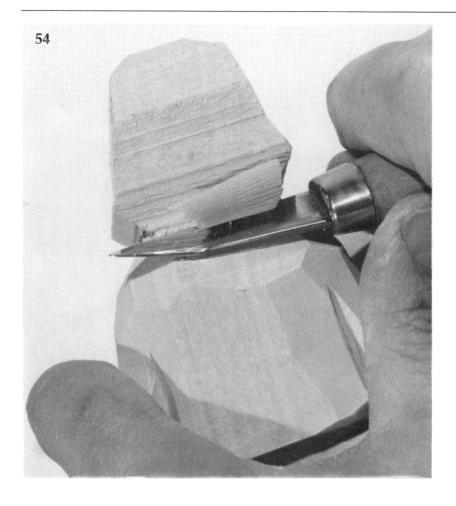

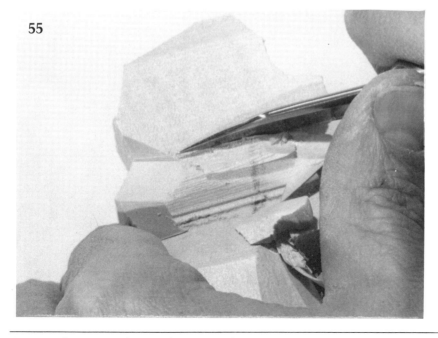

Recess the material under his cap . . .

56

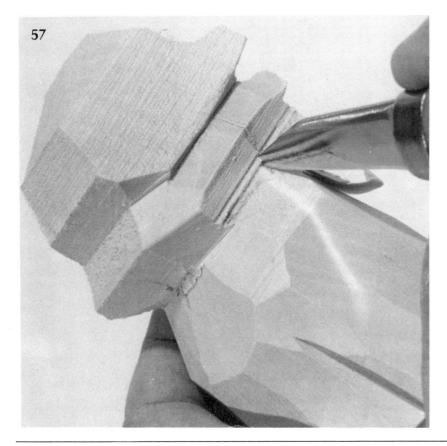

57

Cut in to a depth of about ⅛″ at the front of his hairline.

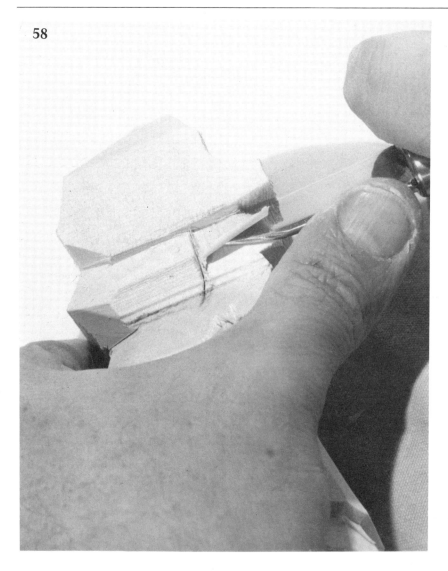

58

Thin the width of his head so that hair is visible on both sides of his head when he is viewed from the front (steps 58 and 59).

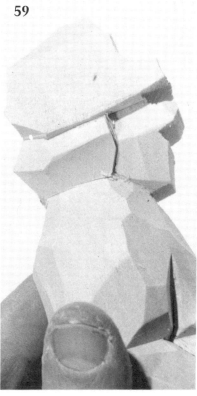

59

60

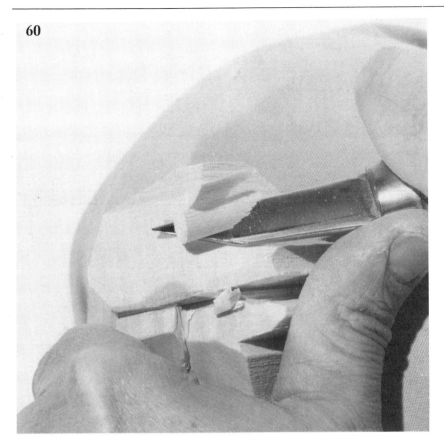

61

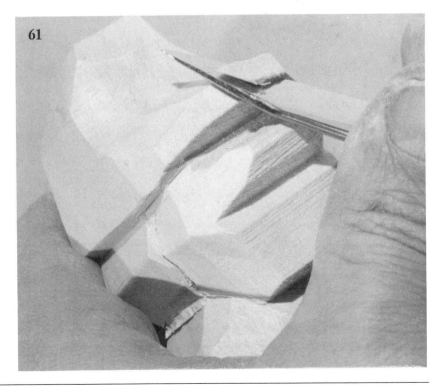

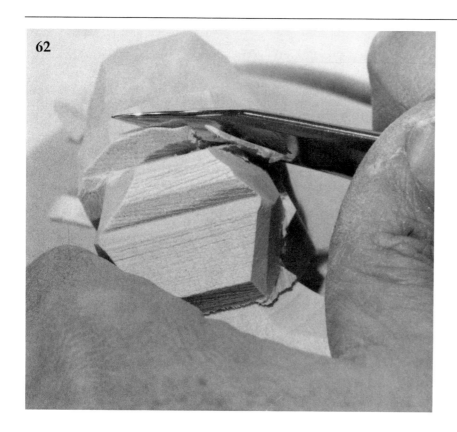

62

Surface the underside as well.

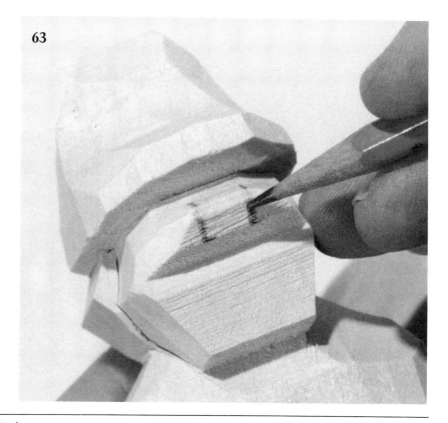

63

Pencil in lines for nose placement.

64

Remove wood from both sides of the nose.

65

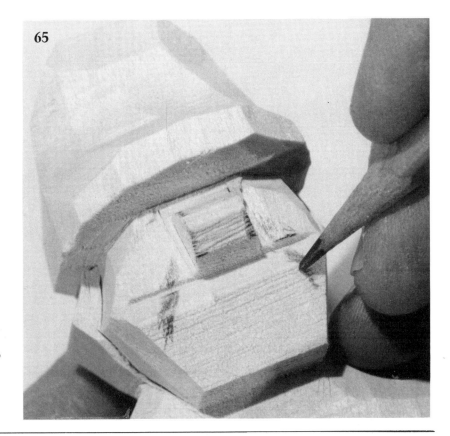

Now for the smile lines, an important element in the face. First, pencil them in. If you'd like a model, look at yourself in a mirror. Note that your smile lines begin at the top of the bulb, or wide part, of your nose, and run downwards and outward, resembling the legs of the letter A.

With the tip of the knife, cut V-cuts where the smile lines were drawn.

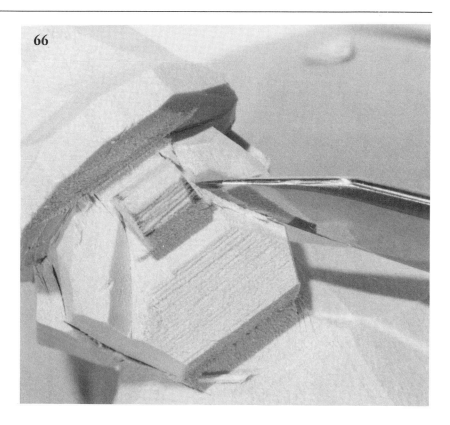

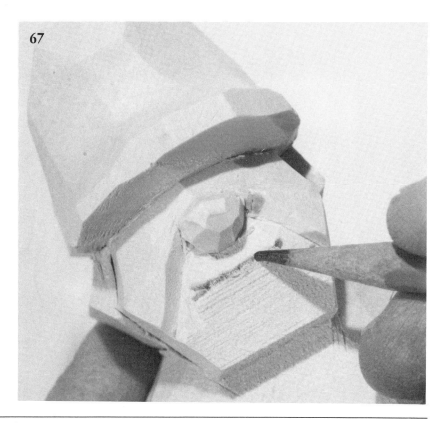

The mouth, usually slightly closer to the nose than the tip of the chin . . .

68

. . . is formed by a horizontal V-cut. The ends of the mouth should almost, but not quite, meet the smile lines.

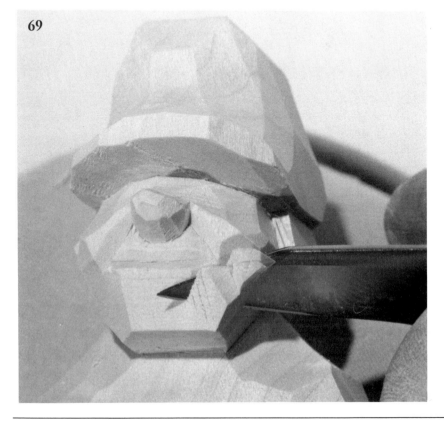

69

Shape the sides of his face . . .

. . . and his chin.

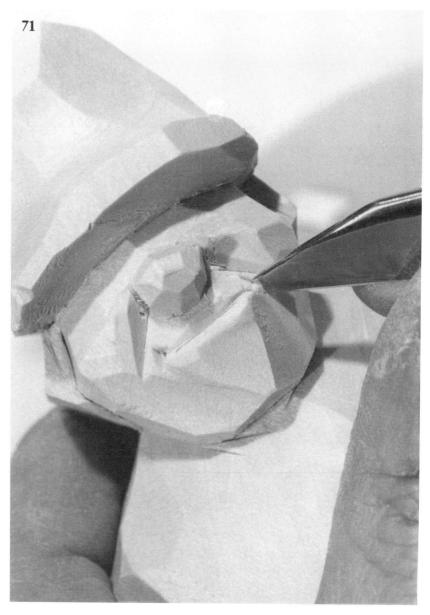

A small triangle at each end of his mouth gives him a slight smile.

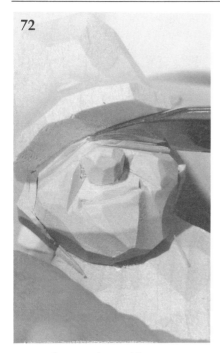

72

Eye sockets are formed by V-cuts.

The eye is formed using the tip of the knife to cut a low, wide triangle, resembling a chip-carving cut. Draw the eyes before you carve them. Avoid making the eyes too small and/or close together, which would render a shifty, beady-eyed look. Again, look in a mirror and note that eyes are spaced about one-eye-width apart and each eye is surprisingly wide. On some people, each eye is nearly as wide as their mouth. Another tip to consider in eye placement: If you were to draw a vertical line downwards from the middle of each eye, the lines would roughly meet the outside corners of the mouth.

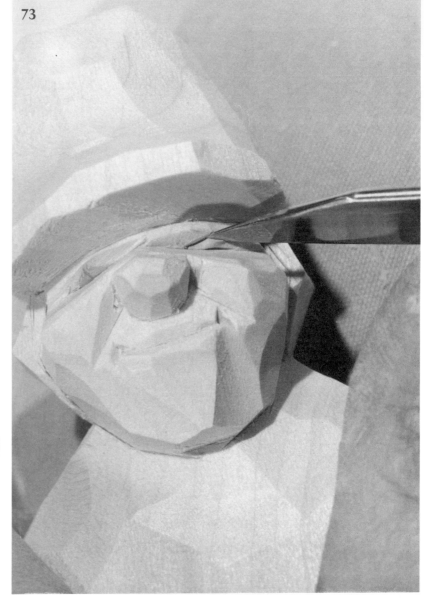

73

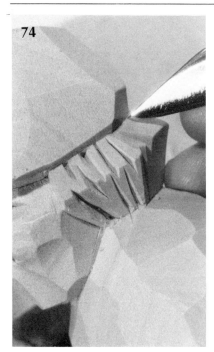

Holding the knife like a pencil, cut in a series of random V-cuts to simulate hair.

A couple of V-cuts at the outside of each eye create crow's-feet.

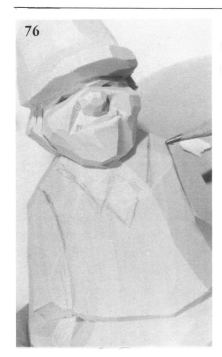

Draw lines to position his shirt collar, V-neck, and sleeves.

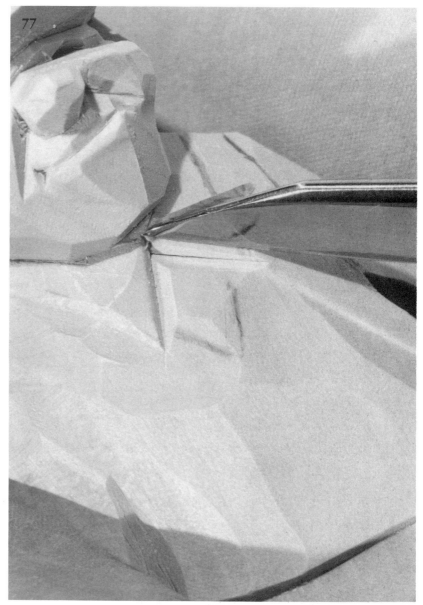

Recess material beneath the collar and where the shirt fits under the sweater, creating different levels (steps 77 and 78).

78

*Rolling the knife while slicing away
from the elbow . . .*

*. . . creates some interesting, final
surface marks.*

The carving is complete.

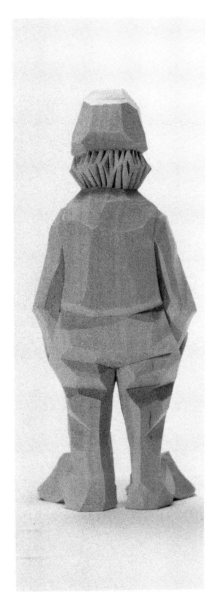

The finished piece.

I color nearly all my figures using acrylic paint that I have diluted with water to form a colored wash or stain. I avoid painting heavily because I want the wood grain to show through, and I prefer using muted earth tones. Thinned oil paints or watercolors can also be used. (While acrylic paints and watercolors are thinned with water, oil paint must be thinned with turpentine or paint thinner.) Very light colors, such as a Caucasian flesh tone as well as white, should be mixed slightly thicker than darker colors to make sure they cover adequately.

Some of my figures have painted rather than carved eyes. As I am carving the face, I create a rounded cavity, or valley, in each eye socket, using a narrow, deep gouge. In painting such figures, the flesh color is painted first. After that color is thoroughly dry, the eyes are painted in. For the eyes, I use the paint at full strength, directly from the container, instead of diluting it with water.

After the paint is completely dry, I liberally coat the figure with boiled linseed oil or Danish oil and then wipe off as much of the oil as possible. To achieve a darker finish, a small amount of dark oil stain (such as walnut or dark oak) or antiquing can be added to the oil. Be sure to add any colorant to the oil very sparingly and to test the resulting mixture on a piece of scrap before applying it to your painted carving.

PATTERNS

$2 \frac{5}{8} \times 1 \frac{3}{4}$

In the patterns that follow, each square equals 1".

Oskar

The step-by-step photos in the previous chapter show you how Oskar is carved. For carvers who have never carved in this flat-plane style or for people who have never carved at all, this figure is an appropriate beginning project. His hands are in his pockets and his ears are covered by hair, relieving the carver of worrying about details while becoming familiar with this style.

As with most of these figures, the colors used for Oskar are muted earth tones. His vest is grey, his shirt is a red iron-oxide, and his cap, pants, and shoes are brown.

Oskar and Sara (see opposite page) were the first in their Scandinavian community to emigrate to America, leading the pack about a century ago.

Sara

After a stormy crossing and a seemingly endless train ride, Oskar and Sara finally arrived at their new home, a recently settled community in western Minnesota.

Here we see Sara wearing the clothes in which she arrived. Her scarf was probably brown or red iron-oxide, her cape dark brown or black, and her skirt brown or dark blue. Since her clothing was undoubtedly made from rather heavy, handwoven material, large flat planes are appropriate for it. Her face can initially be carved in the same way as Oskar's, but then the rough, angular features should be rounded, either with a knife or gouge, to give her a softer, more feminine look. A deeply rounded gouge, approximately ¼" wide, can also be used to make some random vertical grooves in her skirt to create the impression of flowing material.

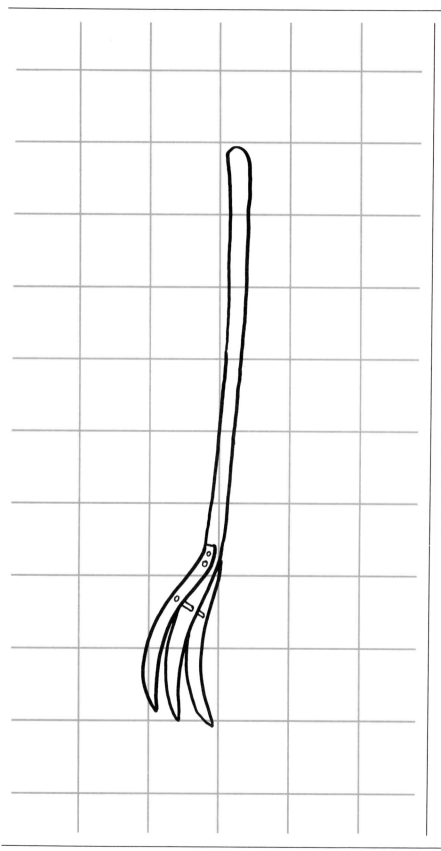

Johannes ✗

Although Oskar and Sara decided to emigrate, nearby cottagers Johannes and Kristina (see next page) were not able to take that step. Their economic plight was no better, but family commitments made the move impossible. However, after a while, their economic conditions did improve, partially because almost half of the population in their community eventually left for the United States or Canada and the pie no longer had to be divided into quite as many pieces.

Johannes is holding a homemade pitchfork, made entirely of wood. Starting with a naturally formed branch that serves as the handle and middle tine, matching tines are then whittled and pegged onto the handle, resulting in a three-tine pitchfork. His left side, with hand in pocket, is carved according to the same general instructions as for Oskar's pocketed hands. When carving his wooden shoes, refer back to the photo on page 18. Once again, dark muted earth tones would be the most appropriate colors.

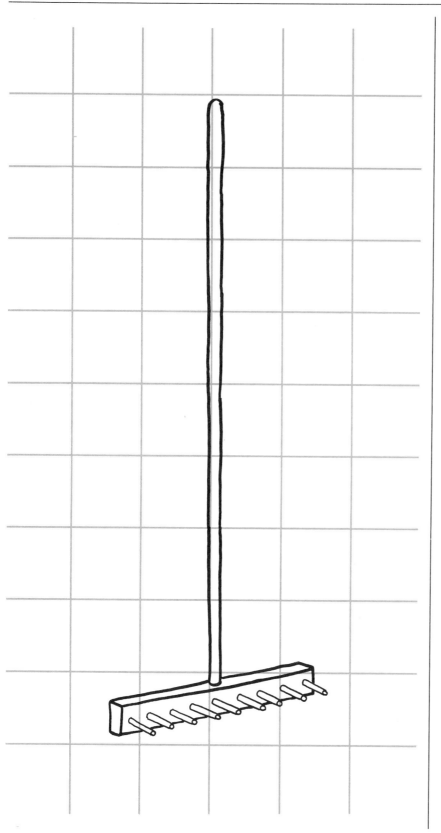

Kristina ✗

Kristina is out raking hay. The handle of her wooden rake is inserted through the ³⁄₁₆″ hole drilled through her right hand. The rake's teeth are whittled pegs inserted into ⅛″ holes in the head of the rake. Kristina's left arm simply hangs at her side. She could be wearing an off-white apron, a dark-green or brown skirt, a beige blouse, and a red iron-oxide scarf.

The Whittler

There is plenty of room on the handle of this laminated Swedish Mora knife, sometimes also referred to as a Swedish carving knife or sloyd knife, to carve something interesting. And if one intends to use the knife for carving or whittling, what better subject could there be than a whittler!

Transfer the shape of the handle onto a practice piece, perhaps a scrap of soft basswood or pine. Carve a prototype to make sure that despite its carved surface, the handle still fits comfortably in your hand. Also, if a different style of knife handle is being carved, facial features and proportions may have to be altered slightly from the pattern presented here.

Warning: Be sure to make a blade guard before beginning to carve the handle (a double thickness of cardboard taped securely around the blade should do nicely).

Once carved, the handle can be painted and/or oiled.

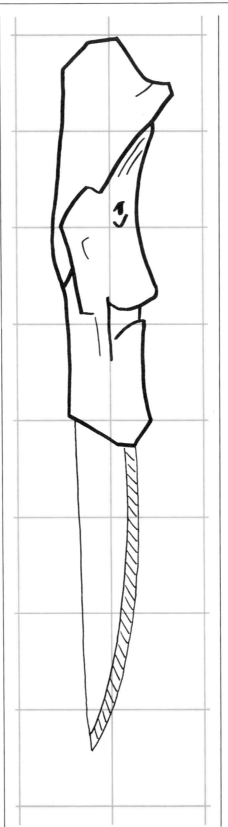

Tomte, or Nisse

The *tomte* (Swedish), or *nisse* (Norwegian), is the bearer of Christmas gifts in Scandinavia. But he and his colleagues are around during other parts of the year as well. Back during the time when most people lived on farms, the *tomte* usually lived in the barn. If treated well, he could be counted on to help around the farm—but if mistreated or scoffed at, the *tomte* could also be mischievous.

This *tomte* has a walking stick in his right hand, not quite as tall as he is, whittled separately and inserted through the hole indicated in the pattern. The hole is ¼" in diameter, but drill a pilot hole first. When drilling the hole, align it so that the walking stick doesn't jab into the top of his foot but touches the ground just beside it.

He also has a homemade backpack woven from birch bark. Using a V-tool or knife tip, carve lines to indicate a basket-weave pattern.

His beard could be white, his cap red (with a red or white ball), his jacket green or red, and his mittens and backpack a golden color. (The white side of the birch-bark strips should face inward.) His shoes could be yellow ochre, brown, or brownish-green, depending on how long and where he has worn them.

Nisse Mor

The *nisse mor* (*mor* means mother) featured here can have a gouge-grooved skirt, described in the instructions for carving Sara on page 97. Note that her face is not rugged and angular but softly rounded. Her hands are tucked under her apron, which can be decorated with stripes or floral designs. Her hat could also be decorated, perhaps with a border near the bottom. The colors could be somewhat brighter than those on an immigrant figure, but earth tones would still be most appropriate.

Third Generation in America

He attends the Scandinavian festivals and celebrations in the Midwest without fail. Nordic Fest, Høstfest, Lutefisk Days, Midsummer—he wouldn't miss them for the world. Although he has never been to the Old Country, he's proud to be one of its sons.

He gets carved in a similar way to the other male figures on the preceding pages. His heels should be close together, with his toes pointing out. To aid in removing wood from between his arms and body, a small hole can be drilled to get started. Color choices could include a muted blue for his bib overalls, red for his shirt, and green for his seed cap. This fellow requires a piece of wood measuring $3'' \times 3'' \times 11''$ but of course can be scaled down if you prefer.

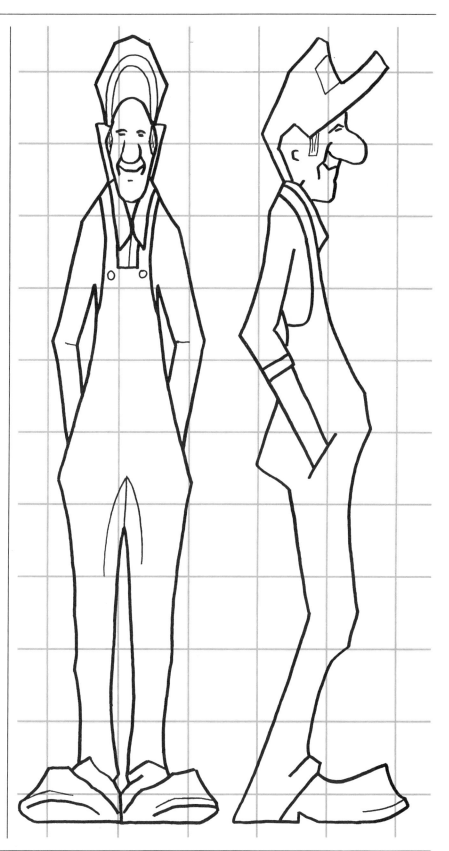

Ice Fisherman

To be able to sit out on the ice like this for hours at a time, one needs to invoke the spirit of St. Halvor the Patient, patron saint of woodcarvers and fishermen.

This fisherman and bucket can be carved as one piece, or the bucket can be sawn off, carved separately, and the figure can be seated on it after the carving is completed. The latter method makes it much easier to access the back and inside of his legs during the carving process.

Carve a separate piece for the fishing pole, and insert it into a 3/16" hole drilled into his hands, as shown. Also, small holes can be drilled into opposite sides of the wide end of the bucket, into which ends of a piece of wire can be inserted, forming a handle.

After having been painted in earth tones (although he could be brightened up a bit with a red scarf) and oiled, he can be mounted on a base of your choice. Drill a tiny (no larger than 1/16") hole through the base, and string a length of elastic thread through the hole. Tie one end to the end of the fishing pole to indicate a fishing line. Draw the thread snugly through the base and knot it underneath. This will give the line a taut look, as if there were a lead sinker or bait on the end.

Woodchopper

This woodchopper is determined. No hair is visible on him, since his arms touch the sides of his head and only his cap shows from the back because it runs all the way down to his collar. His hands should be left large and stylized to provide ample material for the hole (marked with dotted lines) through which the axe handle will go. After drilling a tiny pilot hole through his hands, enlarge the hole to ¼". Once the axe is carved, cut off about ½" of the axe handle (the flared end) and insert it into the hole from the top of the carving. The axe should be inserted so that the head is down and near his back. This position guarantees a powerful swing. One way you can create buttons on this figure is to drill holes (no larger than ³⁄₁₆") and insert round, whittled pegs.

Logger

The timber stands of the upper Midwest, Pacific Northwest, and Canada provided employment for countless Scandinavian immigrants, such as Karl. Here, he's holding a cant hook, which can be carved separately and inserted through a $\frac{5}{16}''$ hole drilled through his hands, as shown. The wooden cant-hook handle can be either left unpainted or painted a dark-yellow ochre. The metal fittings on the cant hook can be steel-blue or grey. Karl could be wearing a black cap, red shirt, brown trousers, off-white or grey socks, and dark-brown boots.

Bringing in the Firewood

Walter, here, has no time to stop for anything. He's got to bring in the wood—one of the most important chores of the day.

Carve the figure without his cargo. This allows access while carving his face (which is visible from the side even after the firewood is added) as well as his chest, the top of his arms, and the inside of his mittens.

After painting the figure in colors of your choice, add the pieces of firewood, which are carved individually and glued together in his arms.

Reading

Even though her days were filled with hard work, Eva savored those moments when she could sit down with a book. One of her brothers worked on a ship, and through her reading she got to travel with him, sailing to exotic ports of call, brimming with sunshine and fresh fruit.

The log bench is carved separately. Drill four ¼″ holes into the log seat, as indicated, and insert the whittled legs.

Paint her clothing in muted earth tones of your choice.

Nisse

As with his Swedish cousin, the *tomte*, this Norwegian *nisse* is the bearer of Christmas gifts in his country. Dressed quite regally here, he looks almost like Father Christmas, with his red coat and hat trimmed with white. His beard and hair are also white, but different texturing on the hair will distinguish it from the trim. (Use a V-tool on the hair and a small rounded gouge to texture the trim.) His clogs can be painted yellow ochre, darkened slightly with brown.

The Schoolteacher

Miss Barrows began teaching in a one-room country school when she was seventeen, and she continued teaching in various schools for the next hundred years. At least, that's what it seemed like to her pupils. She could be tough, but her severity was tempered by those occasions when she would hold the entire second grade (both of us) on her lap during reading. She usually wore a black or dark-brown skirt and an off-white blouse.

Down a Quart

This is Sparky, a gas-station attendant of an earlier era. He was there to fill the tank, check the oil and tires, clean your windshield, and fill you in on everything from driving conditions and weather reports to sports scores.

His pants can be painted either blue or olive-green. His shirt and cap, perhaps featuring the logo of your favorite service station, can be painted white or "company colors."

The Gardener

When May rolls around, Gus gets his hoe out of the tool shed and begins to commune with nature, carefully tending those plants and seedlings he's been thinking about since February.

Drill a ³⁄₁₆″ hole through his hand and insert the hoe, which is carved separately. The blade of the hoe can also be carved separately and then glued onto the handle.

Outfit him in subdued colors of your choice. You may want to paint the metal portion of the hoe a bright color, such as blue, green, or red.

Alleluia

Rev. Carlson has a rather firm grip on his emotions. You'll probably never see him doubled over with laughter or shouting loudly and inappropriately. But what is more important is that he's there through thick and thin—celebrating, grieving, tending his flock.

His clerical shirt is black, with a white collar. Using either glue or wood screws, mount the bust on a wooden base of your choice.

The Bird Watcher

Just as some dog owners eventually begin to resemble their pets, the beak on this bird watcher is becoming more pronounced with each passing migration.

A khaki-colored uniform would be appropriate. The pith helmet and socks are off-white, the shoes are brown, and the binoculars are black.

The Auditor

"I'm here to take a look at your books." Dressed in a black or dark-blue suit, this auditor presents a severe image.

His briefcase, sawn from ½"-thick stock, can be carved separately. Drill a ³⁄₁₆" hole through his hand to accommodate the handle, which can be made from either two pieces of wood, carved and glued into place, or from a piece of leather shoelace. If you prefer the leather handle, drill two ⅛" holes into the top of the briefcase; then thread a leather shoelace, cut the appropriate length, through his hand and glue both ends into the holes in the briefcase.

Ale Hen Candle Holder

The design for this candle holder is based on a traditional Scandinavian ale hen, described in Chapter 1. Band-saw the piece from 1⅛"- to 1¼"-thick basswood or pine. Sand the entire piece; then V-tool in the design as shown. Drill a ¾" vertical hole (or appropriately larger, if you will be using brass candle-holder inserts, available from woodcraft suppliers) for the candle. The piece can be left natural (finished with satin varnish or oil) or can be painted in colors of your choice.

Holiday Candle Holder

Saw this piece to shape from ⅜″-thick stock. Drill a vertical hole to accommodate a birthday candle, as indicated. (Based on the size of the candle you will be using, the hole should be approximately ³⁄₁₆″.) Surface-carve the entire figure; then V-tool in his features as shown. His beard as well as the base can be painted white. His robe is red, and his cap and mittens can be either red or bright green.

Letter Opener

Saw the letter opener from ¼" or
³⁄₁₆" material. Carve the head as
shown, using a V-tool for detail in
his beard, hat, and hair. In shaping
the blade, imagine a two-edged
knife blade. The center remains
thicker, but it thins down to form
cutting edges on both sides. Paint
the cap red and the trim and beard
white. The blade can either be
painted or left a natural-wood
color.

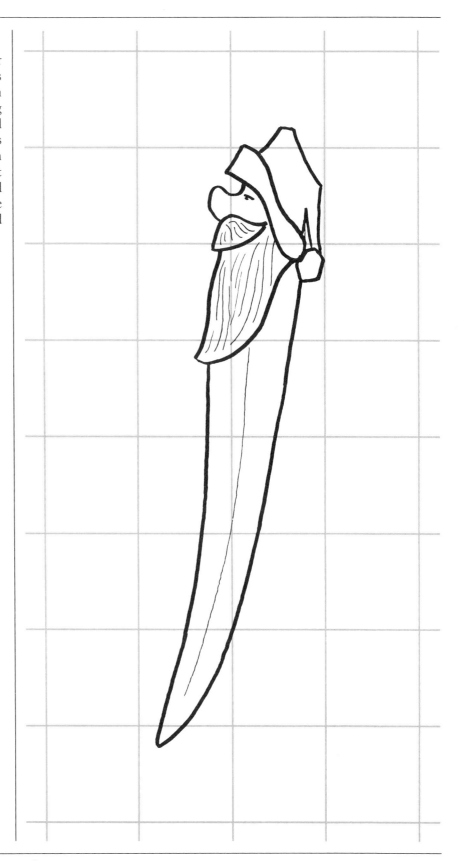

Ornaments

The holiday ornaments here and on the following pages are sawn from ¼" material. Drill a 1/16" hole through each ornament; the dot on the patterns indicates hole placement. Later, thread a cord through the hole to hang the ornaments on a tree.

Surface-carve the front side, and sand the back. (Or, if you prefer, you can carve both sides.) Carve off the sharp corners so that the ornament resembles a cookie.

V-tool the design; then paint with appropriate holiday colors. Since I want my Christmas ornaments to help create a bright, festive atmosphere, I don't thin the acrylic paint with as much water as when I'm painting muted turn-of-the-century immigrant figures.

Finally, wooden stands can be made so that the ornaments can be placed on a shelf or table instead of hung on a tree. Rip a ¾"-wide strip (lengthwise) from a standard ¾" pine board. Then, using either a shaper or table saw, cut a ¼"-wide groove ¼" deep the entire length of the strip. Saw the strip into pieces approximately 2" long. Sand the pieces on all surfaces, and they will make ideal stands for your ornaments.

Sledder

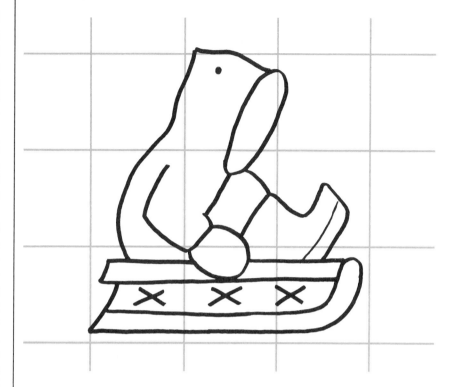

Home for the Holidays

Christmas Morning

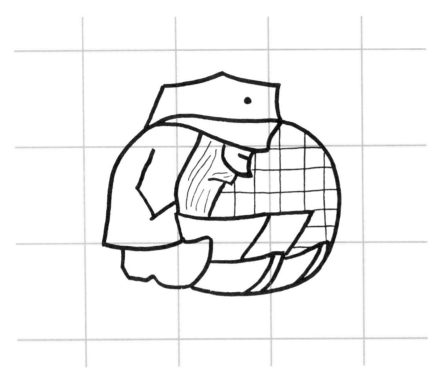

Christmas Goose

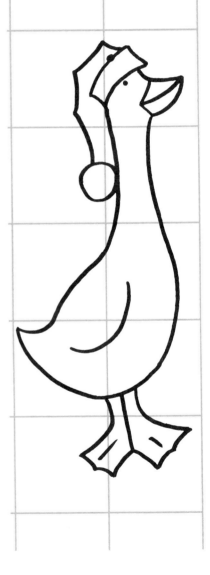

Mounted Nisse

The Christmas Story

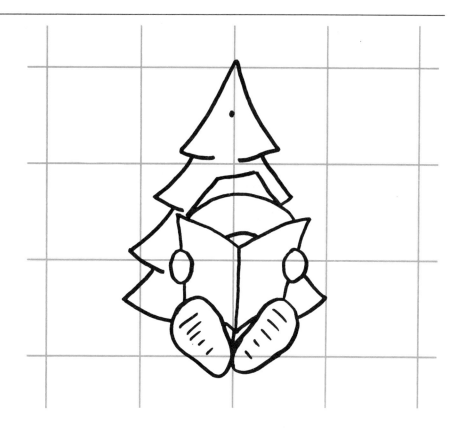

Tomte

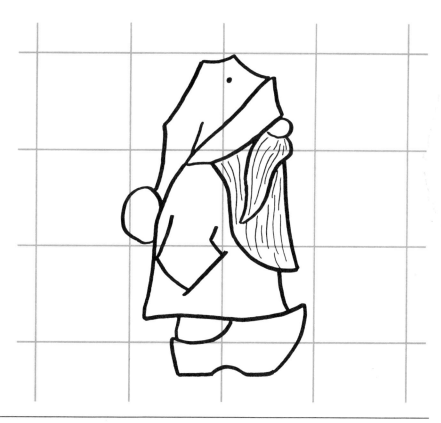

METRIC CONVERSION

Inches to Millimetres and Centimetres

MM—millimetres   *CM—centimetres*

Inches	MM	CM	Inches	CM	Inches	CM
⅛	3	0.3	9	22.9	30	76.2
¼	6	0.6	10	25.4	31	78.7
⅜	10	1.0	11	27.9	32	81.3
½	13	1.3	12	30.5	33	83.8
⅝	16	1.6	13	33.0	34	86.4
¾	19	1.9	14	35.6	35	88.9
⅞	22	2.2	15	38.1	36	91.4
1	25	2.5	16	40.6	37	94.0
1¼	32	3.2	17	43.2	38	96.5
1½	38	3.8	18	45.7	39	99.1
1¾	44	4.4	19	48.3	40	101.6
2	51	5.1	20	50.8	41	104.1
2½	64	6.4	21	53.3	42	106.7
3	76	7.6	22	55.9	43	109.2
3½	89	8.9	23	58.4	44	111.8
4	102	10.2	24	61.0	45	114.3
4½	114	11.4	25	63.5	46	116.8
5	127	12.7	26	66.0	47	119.4
6	152	15.2	27	68.6	48	121.9
7	178	17.8	28	71.1	49	124.5
8	203	20.3	29	73.7	50	127.0

BIBLIOGRAPHY

"Axel Peterrson Döderhultarn" and "Det Är Något Särskilt med Trä," articles in *Hemslöjden 1991/2* (pp. 9–11) (written in Swedish). Stockholm: Olle Nessle and Mark Esping, 1992.

Henning, Darrell; Marion Nelson; and Roger Welsch, *Norwegian-American Wood Carving of the Upper Midwest* (written in English). Decorah, Iowa: Vesterheim, 1978.

Magerøy, Ellen Marie, *Norsk Treskurd* (written in Norwegian, contains English summary). Oslo: Det Norske Samlaget, 1983.

Nylén, Anna-Maja, *Swedish Handcraft* (English translation of *Hemslöjd*, written in Swedish). Lund: Håkan Ohlssons Förlag, 1976.

Rådström, Anne Marie, *Dalahästen* (written in Swedish). Hedemora: Gidlunds Bokförlag, 1991.

Weissman, Ira, and John Matthews, *Master American Woodcarver Emil Janel* (written in English). New York: New York Woodcarving Press, 1984.

INDEX

ABOUT THE AUTHOR

Harley Refsal teaches Scandinavian Studies at Luther College in Decorah, Iowa, where he also holds the title Resident Fellow in Scandinavian Folk Art. He is an internationally recognized figure carver, specializing in Scandinavian-style flat-plane carving.

Refsal was born and raised on the farm near Hoffman, Minnesota, homesteaded by his Norwegian-immigrant grandparents. He began working in wood as a young boy. His father, a carpenter and farmer, and a woodworker uncle who lived nearby kept him well supplied with wood, tools, and encouragement.

Primarily self-taught, Refsal began winning awards in regional and national carving exhibitions by the late 1970s. He also began researching the history of Scandinavian flat-plane carving, with which he had become especially enamored. But soon he discovered that most of the artists who had worked in this style during the height of its popularity earlier in this century in both Scandinavia and America had died and the tradition of flat-plane carving had faded to near-extinction.

Since the 1980s, Refsal, who speaks fluent Norwegian, has shared his knowledge of, and skills in, Scandinavian flat-plane carving with thousands of carvers in classes and presentations in the United States and Scandinavia. His name is so integrally linked with the revival of this carving style that it is rapidly becoming known as the "Refsal style."